Liat can always be depended on for anything, because she is so incredibly responsible. We have her to thank for many of our fun activities this year! Liat is full of ruach and her cheerful manner brightens the lives of everyone she comes in contact with. It is truly admirable how Liat manages to be inclusive of everyone, and we know that this middah will take her very far in life. Liat, keep living a life filled with ruach!

We will miss you! Love your friends
and The Morot
Class of 2021

TOO BEAUTIFUL

TOO BEAUTIFUL

Stories So Uplifting They Had to Be Shared

by

Hanoch Teller

New York City Publishing Company
a division of M.E.T. llc

12   10   8   6
    11   9   7   5

Library of Congress Cataloging-in-Publication Data

Teller, Hanoch.
   Too beautiful: stories so uplifting they had to be shared / by
Hanoch Teller.
      p. cm.
      ISBN 978-1-881939-20-7 (hardcover: alk. paper)
      1. Jewish way of life--Anecdotes. 2. Jewish exempla. 3. Jews--
Anecdotes. 4. Rabbis--Anecdotes. I. Title.
BM723.T4435 2009
296.7--dc22   2009040829

Distributed by
FELDHEIM PUBLISHERS   J. LEHMANN
200 Airport Executive Park   Unit E Viking Industrial Park
Nanuet, NY 10954   Rolling Mill Road
FELDHEIM PUBLISHERS   Jarrow Tyne & Wear
POB 35002   NE32 3DP UK
Jerusalem, ISRAEL
www.feldheim.com

Also by
Hanoch Teller

Once Upon a Soul
Soul Survivors
'Souled!'
The Steipler Gaon
Sunset
Courtrooms of the Mind
Above the Bottom Line
Pichifkes
The Bostoner
"Hey, Taxi!"
Bridges of Steel, Ladders of Gold
The Best of StoryLines
Give Peace a Stance
A Matter of Principal
A Midrash and a Maaseh
Welcome to the Real World
13 Years
And from Jerusalem, HIS Word
It's a Small Word, After All
THE MINI A Midrash and a Maaseh
In an Unrelated Story...
Builders
О Том Что На Душе
Героизм Нашей Души
ועמך כולם...
בצדק תשפט
Érase Una Vez
Desde Jerusalem...
Do You Believe in Miracles? (DVD)
The Righteous Live On (audio cassette and CD series)
Comprehending the Incomprehensible
(CD series)
Building Bene Brak (CD series)

APPROBATION OF
HARAV ASHER WEISS Shlita

אשר זעליג וייס

כגן 8

פעיה"ק ירושלם ת"ו

בס"ד

תאריך _____

לכבוד ידידי היקר והנעלה

הרב היקר והנכבד

הרב הגאון שליט"א הי"ו

שמחתי לשמוע על ספר הנכבד והחשוב בדיני אבילות לאור. ראוי ונכון גם כמינין
יצדק לקהותיו אשר גדלה אך מאומה חשובה, נעימה, ינוחת הביאור, ונוחות
אך כל הענינים האישים ונעלמות אך הדברים הנכבד הגל ונכון לינוך ונכבד לרבות, והנעלם הקושט
ונעלה.

הנני לברך לבבם לבד וכל הנכנס הינה כולם לרבות בכבוד ראוי דרכו הנעלה כי לשמי, לכוח
ברכת היל.

בברכה נדיבה

אשר וייס

APPROBATION OF
HARAV CHAIM MENDEL BRODSKY Shlita

RABBI C. M. BRODSKY
ROSH HAYESHIVA

YESHIVA GEDOLAH ZICHRON SHMAYAHU
567 LAWRENCE AVENUE WEST
TORONTO, ON M6A 1A5

בס"ד

מ"ג יסי רמב', א"

לכבוד ידי' ואוהבי, יקר ונעלה הרב חיים שלי פעל'ן,

נ"א'ם ג', אלה הפעולות' לבו אאברי ברכה לכ"ק

ועל וזאר פסו חדש פג', וכן פפעו, הקואיא

כ'ו יפ' לפעל', לאוע וחעלו לחוך לפואל של

קורון, יטוא את רוח וקראו לסואל פעלא,

בבר שואתת ... הרב האמער פע' ולבג ע', פס'ו

וריזותו הפולטוא לחפך אלו פלאבות לואוע', לפלוף,

לואצת ה' ... ולעא ולפר האבות.

וה"נ פפל ה' ... לאואר ע'נהב ען

קוש' פסו חדש הנאא והפלא ילבב בפוואתו

הארוכים לאאיק לאואת הפוי לבראא קץ האורא

ולברא' ... הקדש, ... לפ'

ל'נעו פלפ ...

ברצות אול ואברכה פקעל ...

חוא אלף ברושא...

APPROBATION OF
HARAV AARON LOPIANSKY Shlita

בס"ד

Rabbi Aaron Lopiansky
ROSH YESHIVA

הרב אהרן לאפיאנסקי
ראש ישיבה

ישיבה גדולה דוואשינגטאן
YESHIVA GEDOLAH OF WASHINGTON

Tishrei 5770

Rabbi Chanoch Teller has once again graced us with a book full of inspiring stories. Our rebbi, Hagaon Rebbi Chaim Shmulevitz would be critical of many of the story tellers, stating "the stories do not describe the gadol, rather the qualities of the gadol define the story". He meant that a great person is not merely a collection of noteworthy deeds, but rather someone whose deeds have a non emulatable dimension, the unique imprint of his person. Rav Chanoch has an uncanny ability to capture a defining moment in great people's – and "ordinary" people as well- lives. These flashes of great insight teach something about the soul of the deed rather than merely the events per se.

This book will continue to inspire many, and may the author merit continuing his holy task of harbotzas hatorah, in the many ways that he does so.

בברכה

אהרן שרגא הלוי לופיאנסקי

1216 Arcola Avenue Silver Spring, MD 20902 w Phone: 301.649.7077

Contents

Foreword
MA'ASIM TOVIM FOUNDATION

EDUCATORS, PHILOSOPHERS, and wise people all agree that *'a picture is worth a thousand words.'* The *Dwner Maggid* expanded on this axiom, by adding: "A good story can drive a message home, quicker and better than many a *Mussar Schmuess.*"

"There's nothing that restores the soul, purifies the heart, deepens one's thinking, and brings one closer to his/her Father-in-Heaven — than storytelling," wrote Rabbi Nachman of Breslav. "You need proof? Review the Pentateuch, the Five Books of Moses. The *Ribbono Shel Olom* prefaced the Story of Creation before all the commandments of the *Torah.*" And he continued: "People say, 'stories are an excellent inducer of sleeping;' and I say, 'good stories awake people from their slumber...' Stories propel us from apathy to empathy.

Adds Rabbi Sholom Dov Ber, the Middle Lubavicher Rebbe: "One needs intelligence to know how to recite a story; but one needs even more intelligence to know how to listen to the right story; and then internalize it, in order to propel us to action.

The Infinite Power of the Story

No one articulated it better than the Ba'al Shem Tov, the founder of *Chassidus*: "When Chassidim assemble in harmony and brotherhood, and recite events and/or activities of the righteous, *HaShem* above views such recitals with the same degree of holiness, as if they were laboring and crouching over the most complex of scholarly material.

The renaissance of Jewish literature and publications in the post-Holocaust era, has produced many talents of Jewish thought, essays, and volumes of writings on a myriad of *Torah* subjects, both in Hebrew and in English. Many previously mysterious subjects have been deciphered, expounded upon, and made accessible.

Baruch HaShem, we have more *Yeshivahs* and *Bais Yaakovs* than ever. More and more young men choose learning as a way of life, and our future mothers study more *Hash'ko'foh* and *M'for'shim,* and know more *Ramban's* than in previous generations. Yet we live in a paradoxical era: We have more conveniences, but less time. We have conquered outer space, but not inner space. We have cleaned up the air, but polluted the soul. We have split the atom, but not our prejudices. We have multiplied our possessions, but reduced our values.

A Person who knows all the answers,
most likely misunderstood the questions

These are days of quick trips, disposable diapers, and pills that do everything from cheer, to quiet, to *chas v'cha'lila,* the unmentionable. We have learned to rush, but not to wait. We have higher incomes, but lower values. We have more acquaintances, but fewer friends. We build more and more computers to hold more information, produce more copies than ever, but we have less communication. We have become long on quantity, but short on quality.

These are days of two incomes, but more divorce; fancier houses, but broken homes. These are times of relative world peace, but more domestic warfare. We have more kinds of food, but less nutrition. We spend too recklessly, get too angry too quickly, stay up too late, and get up too tired. We have more knowledge, but less judgment. We have more experts, but more problems; more medicine, but perhaps less wellness.

We have wider freeways, but narrower viewpoints; taller buildings, but shorter tempers. We talk too much, but truth is rarer than ever. We spend more, but we have less. We may have all come to these shores on different ships, but we are in the same boat now.

Some Say, "It's true that hard work never killed anybody,
— but I figure, why take a chance?"

Perhaps, we need to reset some priorities: Hard work is the yeast that raises the dough…We must place quality ahead of quantity. *Kiddush HaShem* above selfishness. *Ehrlich'keit,* to keep pace with *frum'keit.* Integrity rather than dishonor and deviousness.

*At the close of the Civil War, Robert E. Lee was offered the Presi-
dency of a large insurance company. Lee replied that he did not
feel his services would be worth the $50,000.00 salary offered.*
  *"We aren't interested in your services," the man replied. "We
merely want your name." "That," said General Lee quietly, "is
not for sale."*

Of course, we can be complacent, and console ourselves with the
tremendous accomplishments of our generation, in *Torah* learning,
charitable activities, and many wonderful supportive organizations. Yes,
there is much to be proud of. A great statesman once said, "Life's most
persistent and urgent question is: 'What are you doing for others?'" The
ultimate measure of a person is not where one stands in moments of
comfort and convenience, but where we stand at times of challenge and
controversy. One of the most popular American presidents phrased it
this way: "There are risks and costs to action; but they are far less than
the long-range risks of comfortable inaction."

Along comes the King of Story Tellers, to make another dent on
our collective consciences, to propel us to greater heights of selfless-
ness and caring. *Hanoch Teller's* reputation precedes him, not only from
his previous best-sellers that are already being cherished by two generations, but also from his many deep-thinking and challenging talks
at *Shabbatons* and other community gatherings. *Hanoch's* motto has
always been, 'the time is always right, to teach and to do what is right.'

The first task at hand is to shower fresh buckets of joy unto the
reader. Happiness and joy are the prerequisites in the performance of all
the *mitzvahs*. *Hanoch Teller* is uniquely qualified for this task. Theodore
Roosevelt writes, "For unflagging interest and enjoyment, a household
of children — if things go reasonably well — certainly makes all other
forms of success and achievement lose their importance by compari-
son." The *Tellers'* beautiful family is an endless wellspring of perpetual
joy, which permeates and radiates through every page of *Too Beautiful*.

However, in order to be uplifted by the boundless joy contained in
this book, one must be open-minded and receptive. Here is a short anecdote to drive the point home:

*A great Japanese Master was visited by a junior professor who
came to inquire about the great Master's wisdom. After a brief*

conversation, the Master decided to serve tea. He poured his visitor's cup full, and then kept on pouring. The young professor watched the overflow, until he could no longer restrain himself. "It is overflowing: no more will go in!"

"Just like this cup," the Master said, "you are full of your own opinions and speculations. How can I teach you wisdom, unless you first empty your cup…?"

In dedicating this volume, *Hanoch* asked me to gather my thoughts and draft a 'Foreword.' It is no small task to write a quality article that is to be positioned alongside the Master Storyteller's writings. I am humbled by this request, and intimidated by the process. I remember reading somewhere, 'you don't have to be great to start — but you have to start, in order to be great.'

Time was of the essence. *Hanoch's* instructions were brief and uncompromising:

You have only just a minute,   *You will suffer if you lose it,*
Forced upon you, can't refuse it.   *Give a count if you abuse it.*
But it's up to you to use it,   *Just a tiny little minute,*
            But an eternity is in it.

I was thinking to myself, 'shall I rush *Hanoch's* rush job, before I finish the rush job I was rushing when he rushed in?' I tried to be optimistic, as the optimist who looks forward to enjoying the scenery on a detour…Thus, this 'Foreword' is first and foremost, to your good health, my dear friend Hanoch! May you live for a thousand years, and I be there to count them.

In a full heart there is room for everything,
and in an empty heart, there is room for nothing.

What should I write about in a book of inspiring and uplifting stories? Everyone is trying to accomplish something big, not realizing that life is made up of little things. So I will leave the bigger stories for Hanoch, and I will share several gems with our wonderful readers.

One morning I was walking along the shore. As I looked down the beach, I saw a human figure prancing around like a dancer. I smiled to myself thinking that someone would dance by himself. So I began to walk faster to catch up.

As I got closer, I saw that it was a young man, and he wasn't dancing. He was reaching down to the shore, picking up something and very gently throwing it into the ocean.

As I got closer, I called out, "Good morning! What are you doing?"

The young man looked up and replied, "Throwing starfish into the ocean."

"I guess I should have asked, why are you throwing starfish into the ocean?"

"The sun is up, and the tide is going out — and if I don't throw them in, they will die."

"But, young man, don't you realize that there are miles and miles of beach, and starfish all along it. You can't possibly make a difference!"

The young man listened politely. Then bent down, picked up another starfish and threw it into the sea, past the breaking waves — and said, 'It sure made a difference for that one.'

After a big *Mussar Schmues* to the entire student body, Rabbi Yisroel Salanter would say, "If my entire *drasha* inspired only one person — it was worth it. And if that one person was me — it was still worth it.

People worry about loss of their funds, but they rarely worry about loss of time. Lost funds may return one day. No one has yet discovered a way to recover even one lost day.

Imagine there is a bank, which credits your account each morning with $86,400.00 — but carries over no balance from one day to the next; and every evening the bank cancels whatever part of the amount you failed to use during the day. What would you do? Draw out every penny, every day, of course!

Well, everyone has such a bank. Its name is 'Time.'

Every morning, every person is credited by their bank with 86,400 seconds. Every night, the bank writes off as 'lost' whatever of this time you have failed to invest for a good purpose. It carries over no balance, and it allows no overdraft. Each day the bank opens a new account for you. Each night the account is emptied. If you fail to use the day's deposits, the loss is yours. There is no going back. There is no drawing against tomorrow, or yesterday.

XVIII / TOO BEAUTIFUL

Time flies — but remember, you are the navigator. 'Time wasted' is 'existence wasted.' All the treasures of the earth cannot bring back one lost moment. The best way to 'kill time' is to work it to death...and here is an interesting story for every parent to ponder.

There are those who acquire their World-to-Come,
in one hour (Avoda Zarah 17a)

With a timid voice and idolizing eyes, a little boy greeted his father as he returned from work: "Daddy, how much do you make an hour?"

Greatly surprised, and giving his boy a glaring look, the father said: "Look sonny, not even your mother knows that. Don't bother me now – I am tired."

"But Daddy, please tell me! How much do you make an hour," the boy persisted.

The father, finally giving up, replied: "Twenty dollars per hour."

"Okay, Daddy. Could you loan me ten dollars?" the boy asked.

Showing his restlessness and positively disturbed, the father yelled: "So that was the reason you asked how much I earn, right? Go to sleep, and don't bother me anymore!"

It was already dark, and the father was meditating on what he said, and was feeling guilty. Maybe, he thought, his son wanted to buy something. Finally, trying to ease his mind, the father went to his son's room.

"Are you asleep, son?" asked the father.

"No, Daddy. Why?" replied the boy, partially asleep.

"Here is the money you asked for earlier," the father said, handing him a ten dollar bill.

"Thanks, Daddy!" rejoiced the son, while putting his hand under his pillow, and removing some money.

"Now I have enough! Now I have twenty dollars!" the boy said to his father, who was gazing at his son, in total confusion.

"Daddy, could you sell me one hour of your time?"

Well, we know that failures are divided into two classes: those who thought and never did...and those who did, and never thought... A parent is supposed to be the child's best friend. A real friend is one who walks in, when the rest of the world walks out...We need to remember, that it is good fathers who make good sons... Frequently, rich parents make poor parents...Parents who are always giving their children nothing but the best, may wind up with nothing but the worst. Some parents really bring their children up; others let them down. The accent of our generation may be on youth – but the stress, is still on the parents. As we learn from the laws of a *Ben Sorer U'moreh*, parents should work together as efficiently as two bookends.

And while on the subject of parenting, here's another good one for our dear readers:

The Echo of Life

A father and son were walking up the mountains. Suddenly, the son falls, hurts himself and screams, "Ouch..."

To his surprise, he hears the voice repeating, somewhere in the mountain: "Ouch..."

Curious, he yells, "Who are you?"

He receives the answer, "Who are you?"

Angered at the response, he screams, "Coward!"

He receives the answer, "Coward!"

He looks to his father and asks, "What's going on?"

The father smiles and says, "My dear son, watch me..."

And then the father screams at the mountain, "I admire you!"

The voice answers, "I admire you!"

Again the father screams, "You are a champion!"

The voice answers, "You are a champion!"

The boy is surprised, but does not understand.

Then the father explained: "People call this 'echo', but really this is 'life'. It gives you back everything you say or do. Our life is simply a reflection of our actions.

If you want more love in the world, create more love in your heart. If you want more competence in your team, improve your competence. This relationship applies to everything, in all aspects of life. Life will give you back everything you have given to it. Your life is not a coincidence. It's a reflection of you!" As *Chazal* teach us, in the manner that one deals with others, he/she will be dealt similarly.

And I will conclude with one final story:

A man stopped at a flower shop to order some flowers, to be wired to his mother who lived 200 miles away. As he got out of his car, he noticed a young girl sitting on the curb, and sobbing.

"What's wrong," the man asked the little girl.

"I wanted to buy a red rose for my mother, but I only have 75 cents, and a rose costs two dollars," replied the girl.

The man smiled, and said "Come on in with me. I will buy you the rose."

The man purchased the rose for the little girl, and also ordered the flowers for his own mother.

As they were leaving, he offered the girl a ride home. She said, "Yes, please! You can take me to my mother."

She directed him to a cemetery, where she placed the rose on a freshly dug grave.

The man returned to the flower shop, cancelled the wire order, picked up a bouquet, and drove the 200 miles to his mother's house.

Thank you for purchasing this book. We are sure that it will bring you many hours of enjoyment. Share the joy with your family and friends, and above all, be happy, and do not worry – for worry does not empty tomorrow of its sorrow; on the contrary, it empties today of its strength... Keep hope alive, for hope sees the invisible; feels the intangible; and ultimately will achieve the impossible...

Happy reading!

Avrohom Pinchos Berkowitz
for Ma'asim Tovim Foundation
Isru – Chag Succos, 5770

Introduction

I failed.

I had intended to write this book in nine (business) days, but did not succeed. My next deadline was less ambitious, but also was not attained. Finally, I went for broke, and ten years later, *voila*!

That's right, ten years. Okay, I wasn't actually writing *all* this time (or else you would have suffered a hernia hefting this volume — and one of my primary concerns, dear readers, is your welfare)... but I was formulating. Yes: deeply and constantly formulating.

Over the last decade, there were ample opportunities for second thoughts. The world — especially the rapid conveyance of information — was changing at a dizzying, hyper-accelerated pace. More and more, it seems, people only have sufficient time and attention for sound bites. Quickies. And let's face it: my nature is not to write telegrams. Moreover, the bookstores — those stalwarts that remain — are running out of shelf space, not to mention there are plenty of new kids on the circuit...

I stroked my beard, now more white than merely "elegantly flecked" with grey. And I wondered, worried. Maybe it was time to gracefully retire from short stories?

Whatever my answer logically should have been, one unassailable truth remained front and center. And it was a simple truth, really.

Too beautiful.

The stories that we had amassed — and I use the word royally — were simply too beautiful not to be shared. Or to be reduced to a one-liner, an ephemeral e-mail, or a mental notation.

In just a few pages, you will understand exactly what I mean.

Because these stories are so refreshing, inspirational and motivational — and Providence has placed them in my lap — this Teller has no choice but to tell them.

Leadership and altruism, *kedushah* and self-sacrifice, love and struggle may not be given short shrift — or the storyteller has neglected his trade, and betrayed his calling.

The stories also contain lessons acquired in the search of wisdom — as opposed to informational "factoids" that proliferate everywhere. Truth to tell, information is easy to come by, but real wisdom — perhaps more than ever — plays hard to get.

Since I began with "True Confessions," I'll make another: the title of this volume was hotly debated in the Teller family. I was in favor; my wife, opposed — and our children, thank God, have been blessed with the common sense to automatically side with their mother.

Several rolling-pins and frying-pans to the head later, however, I nonetheless prevailed. (Any of you who know my wife Aidel, *k'shmah kein hee*, are probably now bent over with laughter. She has never, ever, even raised her *voice*, let alone a heavy object, in *anyone*'s direction.) Then again, she also never grew up with the expression the *kallah iz zu shein*. For those of you not Yiddish-conversant, there is a glossary in the rear of the book. Suffice the non-literal translation to be — in one of the most common Yiddish expressions — "the bride is too beautiful!"

The consequence of this debate over the title is that it got me to *really* think about the word "beautiful" — nowadays, a word oft-used (and oft-abused) both in person and on the page. As a result, I suddenly began seeing it in places where I had barely noticed it before. One such example is in *Shacharis,* in the paragraph directly following the *Shema.* Numerous adjectives are employed to describe our affirmation of the Almighty's kingship, culminating in... *"beautiful."* And so I was inspired to use those adjectives, in order, as the names of the chapter titles.

Years ago I posed the following query to the renowned *poseik*, Harav Yisrael Gans: I told him that upon occasion I cannot fall asleep, so I drink a warm potion that my grandmother taught me about, to make myself drowsy. For flavor, I like to add grape juice — but I knew not which blessing to recite over this cocktail.

Replied the Gaon (and I couldn't make this up): "Your problem is that you read too many Hanoch Teller books, and this is what keeps you up at night; we all suffer from the same problem!"*

I was flabbergasted by his warm-hearted compliment and equally appreciative to all the others, all over the world, who have told me of the pleasure, insight, comfort, motivation, and food-for-thought they derived from my works. I am especially gratified to know that my stories raised spirits, uplifted hearts and touched souls during periods of convalescence and times of immense personal struggle and loss.

No doubt Harav Gans was referring primarily to the extraordinary healing power and the transformative nature of stories — including the ones you now hold in your hands.

The age-old tradition of the *maggid* — a title for which I do not qualify, as these were exceptionally pious, learned individuals imbued with the fear of Heaven (though in a quirk of fate, "*maggid*" is the translation of my last name) — was never to relate a story unless it conveyed a lesson. This is an edict I thoroughly embrace.

I have never told or written a story unless

---

* By the way, he ruled "*Shehakol*."

it contained meaning and counsel. My stories may be entertaining or deeply somber, historical or *au courant;* a *shtickel shtick-y* or earnest to the max... but they *always* have a take-home message.

Many Introductions ago, reference was made to the author who would gladly exchange one hundred readers today for one reader one hundred years from now. Such an achievement would speak volumes (pun intended) about the author's skill. It would reveal that he influenced the thoughts and deeds of humanity; that he left his mark upon the world of literature, that he so brilliantly captured a time, a place or a figure that going back to reread his work would pay historical, as well as artistic, dividends. I often think that if I fail to accomplish this, my compositions will only be worthy of wrapping fish. But this is a judgment that I must leave to the Almighty, and to my dear readers — yesterday's, today's, and tomorrow's.

I deeply regret that five beauties that were slated for inclusion into this volume were shelved at the last minute for various technical reasons. I would like for this book to be my final volume of what have been dubbed "soul stories"; yet I know that these five gems (a number that will presumably grow) will forever gnaw at my conscience.

I confess that my last name has provided me with an incentive or an edge (I am honestly not sure which) in this regard, and I do not take this Godsend lightly. My ideas of how to relate a story are old enough to buy their own liquor, but they were largely formed by my mentor, Marsi Tabak *a"h,* who passed away this year. Although not personally involved in this particular book, her hand is in every page. Her felicity of style and masterful way of conveying emotion will forever guide me and I surely felt her presence as I crafted these stories.

I use this segue to acknowledge others as well. In an earlier title I wrote that one of the best parts of writing a book is the occasion it affords to thank those who have been helpful. It has been a long time and I relish the opportunity.

Reb Avrohom Berkowitz has penned a poignant foreword that graces this book; his family's Ma'asim Tovim Foundation has largely enabled *Too Beautiful*'s publication.

Vivien Orbach Smith shouldered a large share of the brilliant and graceful editing of *Too Beautiful*; I wish we would work together more. In the clutch I called upon the good offices of Feldheim Publishers; and for the record, what a pleasure it has been to have worked with Yitzchak Feldheim and Eli Meir Hollander for all these years. With this latest work, they enabled me to tap into the talents of their very gifted crew, most ably headed by Deena Nataf. And for most competently and selflessly heading the American side of operations, I thank my own Nashi and Gabi Teller.

I deeply appreciate the *Gaonim* who took the time to write approbation letters. As a first for me, two of the letters were written by two of my dearest (if I may be so bold) friends, certainly two of my closest mentors. One of them was kind enough to review the entire manuscript and approve the contents.

Meticulous and incisive copy-editing was performed by Elcya Weiss and Rivka Lev. In the twelfth hour, Shragie Bomzer lent his eagle-eyes to proof the galleys and Hannah Hartman did far more than typesetting, as she always does. To verify some of the details in this manuscript, Rabbi Dr. Howie Apfel allowed me to pick his brain for its vast repository of medical knowledge; he could have provided a similar fountain of knowledge on the Talmudic end as well.

Jeremy and the folks at Staiman Design, yet again, hearkened to a last-minute call to execute something appealing, tasteful and within budget. Of late, Yael Etziony has been something of a right hand — occasionally even *two* hands. Her expert assistance is reflected in this work as well.

Gratitude must be expressed to the exceptional men and women who contributed their stories to "Too Beautiful." I equally value the many individuals who shared unforgettable stories with me that could not be included in this particular volume.

The extraordinarily gifted shutterbug, Dr. Diane Medved, took the "too beautiful" photograph that graces this cover. She could make concrete look lush and artistic — and photography is arguably the least in her panoply of talents! For the record, let it be known that I had fully intended to sing her praises here, along with those of her celebrated husband Michael, long before she graciously offered me the cover photo. Foiled again!

No matter. Let the record show my recognition of the Medveds as two brilliant, ringing voices of sanity, courage, and most importantly, *kedushah* in our insane, cowardly, unholy world. I shudder to think what our situation would be if they were not on our team. Continuously, tirelessly and dynamically, the two of them — although Michael in a much more public way — have upheld truth and justice, impacting the lives of millions.

I am also privy to the Medveds' unique generosity and magnanimity. I have had, too, the privilege of learning with them (primarily Diane), and I do not know if I can quantify how much she has taught me.

I am honored that Joseph Telushkin considers me a friend; others would consider it a pesky interference to acquire information, advice, and sagacious opinion. Neil Kerman is another who does not know how to maintain a balanced friendship; he knows only how to give. And these two are not my only pals of that persuasion. Dr. Benjy Krupka and I, if we would admit to our true ages, have a friendship that between us is surely a century old. All right, I exaggerate — but it is more than a jubilee; and despite distance, it is vintage wine.

I bless the day that Refael Leib Rosenberg brought me into his orbit. I, and my children, owe gazillions to Refael and Batya Rosenberg for a gazillion reasons — but very significantly, for introducing me to that giant of *chessed*, the brilliant, gifted and generous Rabbi Gil Frieman. As you shall see in the coming pages, p"G, description is usually not my weakness — but to Gil and Dr. Shulamis Frieman, I cannot even do minimal justice.

I doff my (admittedly dusty upon occasion) hat to Jerry Greenwald of *The Jewish Press* for featuring my monthly column for... gosh, I don't-even-know-how-many years. And paeans of praise I also heap upon Rebbitzen Rochel Kahn, of Camp Tubby fame.

It is no secret that I teach a lot, but I will forever be grateful to Rav Reuven Taragin for shepherding me to my most coveted position, which is delivering a *shiur* in Yeshivat HaKotel. I thank Navah Weiss for overseeing most of the work I do at Yad Vashem.

My former neighbor and forever friend, Jonathan Rosenblum, instills within me (and countless others) wisdom and direction. Similarly, the unbelievably insightful Rabbi Barry Shafier of The Shmuz, who has turned my family and me into insatiable addicts of his engaging *shmuzen*. Rabbi Yisroel Reisman has educated a generation — and continues to do so — and I am one of the many blessed to grow and learn from this master teacher. And by no means leastly, Rabbi Berel Wein is an endless repository of wisdom and *menschlichkeit*. I am privileged (for so many reasons) to live in the same city as Rabbi Wein, and I simply cannot get enough of his original way of delivering his prodigious erudition.

I am aware that I don't thank my kids enough, but I'll give them due credit this time for introducing me to Suzy and Philip Goldberg, my gracious and big-hearted hosts in London. They do an inimitable job, but are nonetheless assisted by the nicest of neighbours (the 'u' is, of course, deliberate), the Jeremy Shebsons and Josy Orensteins. These three families have re-written the book on hospitality, with no editing required — only pages taken, by the rest of us.

Lest I concede a fault and then continue the neglect, allow me to fully acknowledge the blessing of our children. The only thing that I treasure as much are my precious [*gan*] *eidem*s and their distaff counterparts.

I have asserted numerous times that the sweetest people in all of Brooklyn, arguably the world, are Cheskel and Esther Paskesz. I have valiantly sought to apply what I have learned from them in hospitality, and have come up wanting; in fact, I strive to apply what I have gleaned from them in virtually every facet of *bein adam l'chaveiro* and *bein adam l'Makom*... and still cannot manage to walk in their shoes. Yet they still continue to teach me and everyone else who crosses their warm and welcoming path. And so, you see — not only are they the sweetest, but also the most patient.

To my father, the *yeshivah bachur,* you are a treasured example for us all; even when we don't call upon you, you are there for us.

I lift up my voice in gratitude to the Almighty, humbled by all of the grace with which I have been bestowed. The privilege of bringing this book to press is one more, deeply significant, blessing.

In the past, I have concluded with a somewhat boilerplate-ish platitude about the efficacy of stories and a heartfelt wish that my modest contributions will be viewed positively. This time I conclude with a *tefillah* for the healing of those who need to be healed.

Hanoch Teller
Isru Chag HaSukkos 5770
October 11, 2009
Jerusalem תי״ו

Enduring

To Light up the World

A DYNAMO. A powerhouse. Even... "a bulldozer."

This is how they refer to Sima Rabinowitz in her tiny corner of the planet.

Her appearance is inconsonant with this description. Sima is of petite and delicate build, with a voice that while soft and genteel, has a commanding and persuasive quality that few can resist. She has a youthful air, but like many chassidic women in (or slightly beyond) their late thirties, she could also be a grandmother.

Certainly, it is the wisdom and strength of the ages that she brings to her role as the head of women's *chessed* projects in her neighborhood. Several years ago, her tenacity and dedication became the stuff of legend, after a horrific automobile accident devastated the community. There were two fatalities and several who suffered serious injuries, and it was Sima Rabinowitz who was widely credited with preventing this tragedy from erupting into an irrevocable calamity. Overnight, she became a grief counselor, social worker, psychologist, fundraiser and employer, mobilizing agencies and individuals to action in support of the bereaved and struggling families.

She has, they say, the heart of a lion.

IT IS NOT always easy to grow up in the giant shadow cast by such a figure, and this seemed to be the case for Sima's young daughter, Chavi. Though she resembled her mother physically, Chavi was the opposite in personality. She was, from earliest childhood, painfully shy. The next-to-youngest of the eleven children of Sima and Refael Nachman Rabinowitz, Chavi was content to retreat into the comfortable bosom of her family, where she never lacked for playmates. Interacting with others, however, especially adults, was invariably a source of heart-pounding anxiety.

Sima was mindful of the unique nature of each of her children, and understood that Chavi was more sensitive than the rest. But in the area of communal service, there was no compromise. Even at age nine, Chavi was expected to be a foot-soldier in her mother's legendary *chessed* army.

Chavi was none too pleased about this, but there was no negotiating with her mother. "Just do this *chessed*," her mother commanded (in that voice, both firm and compassionate), "and it will open your eyes."

Considering the task Chavi was assigned, it was a choice of words both poignant and prescient.

HER JOB WAS to read to Estelle Leibenson, a blind woman in her sixties, two evenings a week. Sima displayed characteristic wisdom in matching the two, for Miss Leibenson's blindness was, in a sense, an *advantage* to her timid young companion rather than an obstacle to be overcome. Chavi was venturing into the world of *chessed* with tentative baby steps, and the fact that she would not be scrutinized helped make her footing all the more secure.

Miss Leibenson was blind from birth. She had lived for many years in an increasingly rundown neighborhood adjacent to the Rabinowitzes', in the same apartment where she had grown up. Her parents were long gone, marriage and children had passed her by, and she was dependent upon a complex network of social services. She was deeply grateful for assistance, company and conversation.

Bashful Chavi was not adept at making conversation, and during the first few times she came to read to Miss Leibenson, the girl was forced to balance her book on her knees in order to keep her legs from shaking uncontrollably. She would have recoiled in humiliation had her delighted hostess been able to observe her trembling in waves of discomfiture.

Sima's heart would break a little as she watched her daughter reluctantly get ready for these initial visits. The child looked so miserable, so anxious — was this really the right thing? *YES,* Sima would firmly remind herself whenever her own resolve wavered. All *mitzvos* were important... but this one, particularly so. And besides, she had witnessed over and over again, how acts of *chessed* benefit the giver *at least* as much as the receiver.

And that was definitely the case with Chavi Rabinowitz. As she became Miss Leibenson's eyes on a twice-weekly basis, Chavi's confidence blossomed. Her initial fear and resentment evaporated and she actually looked forward to spending time with the woman she now easily called "Estelle," and to alleviating her new friend's loneliness and isolation.

ONE MILD WINTER evening, several months into their relationship, as Chavi was assuming her usual position across from Estelle's reclining chair, the woman sighed deeply. "Two years," she murmured wistfully, "just two more years..."

"Two more years — and what?" Chavi asked hesitantly, curious, but not wishing to pry.

"In two more years," Estelle declared, moving her head slightly from side to side as she often did when she spoke, "I will be able to *see!*"

"WHAT? But... how?"

"That's when I turn sixty-five, with God's help, and become eligible for government assistance. And then I will finally be able to afford the surgery that can correct my vision."

Chavi was thunderstruck. She had no idea that Estelle's lifelong blindness was of a type that could, in fact, be reversed by today's surgical tools and techniques. Of course, the girl was still only nine years old — small wonder that she was not up on the latest in high-tech medicine! But even a *child* could be seized instantly by monumental frustration over what she had just been told, and Chavi thought it to be the most confounding news she had ever heard in her life. *If, indeed, an operation already exists that can confer vision and independence upon Estelle after a lifetime lived in the dark,* she thought, <u>*why*</u> *should the poor woman be forced to wait until she is two years closer to the grave, in order to have it?*

Chavi's childish mind began to swirl, so much so that it became hard for her to recite the text in the strong, clear voice she had acquired since she began visiting Estelle. As of late, her vocal quality echoed that of her irrepressible mother — and now her feverishly determined thought processes mirrored Sima Rabinowitz's, as well. For Chavi was raised in a home where challenges were met head-on, and financial obstacles, in particular, were simply technicalities that could ultimately be resolved. The silent child who had reluctantly accompanied her mother to countless meetings, to the hospital rooms of the sick and the homes of the downtrodden, had clearly absorbed much of her energy.

Chavi Rabinowitz was indeed her mother's daughter. Hardly anybody knew it yet... but it would become clear very, very soon...

THE NEXT MORNING, Chavi stormed into every single classroom of the Bais Yaakov Elementary School she attended — even that of the formidable sixth-graders. The girl who once shrank from her peers, now commanded their rapt attention as she passionately conveyed Estelle's plight. "Look at me!" she ordered. "And now close your eyes, shut them tight — and think of poor Miss Leibenson who has lived this way every day of her life, and who has to *keep on* living this way *only* because she doesn't have money for surgery!"

"'*Lo sa'amod al dam rei'acha*'... do not stand idly by your friend's blood!" she thundered, invoking the Torah's prohibition against complacency when a life hangs in the balance. Her emotional appeal resulted in all the girls rummaging through their coats and backpacks to dig out any change they might have.

By the end of the school day, Chavi had tirelessly solicited every girl in her school. Her fundraising efforts — at least from her adorably naïve perspective — were wildly successful.

Unable to contain her excitement, Chavi headed immediately to Estelle's apartment (even though it was not her regular visiting-time), and burst in with great urgency, startling the bewildered woman.

"Okay, let's GO!" commanded Chavi, in a manner that was quintessential Sima. "Come on, I'll help you put on your coat!"

"But where?" Estelle protested, as Chavi grabbed her arm and attempted to shove it into a bulky sleeve. *"Where are you taking me?"*

At first, Chavi gave no reply, so focused was she on getting Estelle out the door. But, when the fully-grown woman refused to yield, the little girl blurted out her explanation. "I've got the money for your operation, Estelle," she said urgently, "and we mustn't waste *another minute!*"

Estelle was so suddenly caught off guard that she acquiesced to Chavi's determined ministrations, and before she knew what was happening, she was propelled down the stairs, out the door and into the street by a pint-sized powerhouse on a mission.

"Th-th-thank you, dear," she panted, as Chavi steered her at a brisk pace. "But *where exactly* are we going?"

"To an... eye-guy," Chavi confidently announced. Naturally she knew nothing of the important distinctions between optometrists, ophthalmologists — or any other type of physician, for that matter. She only knew that in front of a medical building on the avenue, was a sign that read "All Corrective Eye Surgery." And this, she believed, was precisely what the doctor had ordered.

And so, the unlikely twosome set out into the evening's darkening chill in order to confer with the local ophthalmologist, five blocks away. It did not occur to Chavi that such visits were by appointment only — and that it could take weeks, even months, to get onto a specialist's crowded calendar. But *many* things did not occur to Chavi...

THERE WAS NO training, religious or medical — and Dr. Marty Moskowitz had a good deal of both — that gave the busy ophthalmologist a clue as to what this odd couple was doing in his office. After his final appointment of the day, he beckoned them into an examination room.

It did not take long for Dr. Moskowitz to confirm that Estelle Leibenson's condition was, indeed, amenable to surgery, and he agreed to take her on as a patient. His next available opening, he informed them, was two-and-a-half months hence.

Chavi rejected this news out of hand. "My friend can't wait until then!" she said firmly. "We want the surgery... today!"

"Today?" Dr. Moskowitz repeated, trying to hold back his laughter.

Chavi solemnly waved her hand around the room filled with gleaming stainless steel equipment and the specialized tools of the ophthalmic trade.

"Yes, today!" the child insisted. "We're here, we're ready!"

A second look at Chavi's earnest expression told Dr. Moskowitz that this was no laughing matter. Gently, he explained:

"Young lady, Miss Leibenson needs a complicated surgery called a 'vitrectomy,' and this can only be done in a hospital, not a doctor's office. Also, in order to get medical clearance, she will need to undergo many more tests than the ones I just performed — special imaging tests, heart tests, blood chemistries, and it can take days to get some of the lab results... and then, of course, we'll have to coordinate a surgical team...

"Chavi, do you know what an anesthesiologist is?" he asked.

She shrugged her tiny shoulders.

"Figured as much," Dr. Moskowitz muttered under his breath. "In any case, I only have surgery rights in the operating room one day a week..."

"Well, did you already do a surgery this week?" Chavi questioned eagerly.

"Actually, no — I have a gentleman scheduled for tomorrow. Now, look, I know what you're thinking... but it would be grossly unfair — unethical, even — to cancel a patient who was promised this date..."

"So you can do Estelle right afterwards!"

"Your devotion is very admirable, my dear, but I only get the operating room in the mornings, and the kind of surgery Miss Leibenson needs can take a long time. On her day there can be no other surgery. And remember what I said about the medical tests?

Chavi nodded and tears welled up in her eyes.

"Look," said Dr. Moskowitz wearily, "I give you my solemn word that because of the, ah, unusual circumstances here, I will make this surgery my highest priority. I will order all the preliminary tests to be done immediately, and move Miss Leibenson to the top of my cancellation list. All right, Chavi?"

"All right," she murmured, patting the hand of Miss Leibenson, who sat through this entire exchange in stunned silence.

"Now, as far as payment..." the doctor began, turning his attention to the older woman, who was absorbing the proceedings in a state of shock.

"Oh, it's all taken care of," Chavi chimed in, handing him a bulging envelope.

Moskowitz peered inside.

"How did you get this?"

"It's everything I saved from birthdays and Chanukah *gelt,* and from some money I get for watching my baby brother," Chavi replied, blushing. "But a lot of it," she continued excitedly — lowering her eyes lest she appear conceited — "is what I collected at my school."

"I see," said Dr. Moskowitz, riffling through the coins and the thick sheaf of crumpled bills.

Turning to the older woman, he asked, "Miss Leibenson, does your current health insurance cover short-term hospitalization?"

"I *think* it does," Estelle replied uncertainly.

Moskowitz was silent for a few moments. He carefully placed the envelope inside the pocket of his lab coat.

"Miss Leibenson, I'm sure you have many questions, and I shall answer them all. For now, let me assure you that the discomfort will be manageable, and if everything is successful — which I expect it will be, God willing — you will begin to have sight only a few days after the operation. Meanwhile my office assistant will schedule everything and help you to fill out all the necessary forms."

For the first time since she was commandeered from her apartment, Estelle Leibenson broke into a huge smile of relief. It had all happened so fast! She couldn't believe at first that the miracle for which she had prayed all of her life was finally in her grasp. But it was, thanks to a little girl who had been raised on mother's milk of *chessed.*

A MERE NINETEEN DAYS after Chavi

had marched her into Dr. Moskowitz's office, Estelle was admitted to Long Island Jewish Hospital. Her surgery was an unqualified success. She recovered beautifully, and sailed through vision rehabilitation with flying colors.

Seeing the world and all of its colors for the first time was overwhelming. She was reborn.

The very first place that Estelle ventured out unaided after her recovery, was to the Rabinowitz home. She was surprised to see that Sima Rabinowitz, of the strong voice and oversized personality, was so delicate of appearance.

But her surprise was nothing compared to Sima's.

Somehow, the monumental news of Estelle Leibenson's life-changing surgery had failed to reach the *chessed* captain who had so generously helped for years to coordinate her care. Sima was dumbfounded. *Estelle could SEE?*

"You didn't know?" Estelle gasped. "But

how could you *not* know... it's all thanks to your Chavi!"

If the first shock wasn't earth-shattering enough, the second surely was.

"My... Chavi?"

"That's right — your amazing Chavi!"

Now it was Sima Rabinowitz's turn to process this multi-part miracle. The possibility that her nine year old — the least assertive of all her children — had even the slightest role in Estelle's medical metamorphosis was beyond her comprehension. Motioning to Estelle to join her at the table for a celebratory snack, Sima listened in disbelief as the older woman explained, point by point, how Chavi had orchestrated everything.

As the tale unfolded, Sima felt like she was listening to a fairy tale about the feisty little girl who single-handedly slays a dragon. How on earth could her Chavi have raised the five-figure sum to underwrite this procedure? It was a task that would daunt the most seasoned organizational head!

After Estelle Leibenson took her leave, Sima discreetly launched her own behind-the-scenes investigation and the full story was revealed. In fact, a huge balance remained on this medical bill. It was, indeed, a fairy tale — a fractured one.

If only Chavi had consulted me! Sima thought reproachfully. *Things needn't have turned out this way.* A specialist within Sima's elaborate network of professional contacts might well have performed the surgery at a significantly reduced fee.

But it was too late for that now. As proud as she was of her daughter's unexpected gumption, Sima Rabinowitz dreaded confronting Dr. Moskowitz about paying down the staggering debt. She had no wish to insult this practitioner by haggling over the cost of services he had already rendered in good faith. But dealing with precisely such issues was part of her role as a community leader. Reluctantly, she went to Moskowitz's busy office, and like her pint-sized progeny before her, waited until the last patient had gone, in order to state her case.

At first, Sima was tempted to tell the

good doctor how *sweet* the entire story was — for it truly was — but she did not want to appear to make light of it. Finally, with characteristic bluntness, she took a deep breath and put her cards on the table.

"...As I explained, doctor, I was *completely unaware* of what my little girl had arranged. Naturally, I am most grateful that you were able to grant sight to Miss Leibenson, and I realize that a great deal of money is owed you. I only ask that you put us on a long-term payment plan. The longer it can be spread out, the more likely we will be able to honor our commitment. What about, say... thirty years?"

"Like mother, like daughter," Dr. Moskowitz thought, allowing himself a chuckle. "Mrs. Rabinowitz, I must tell you that this has been the most extraordinary transaction of my career. How often does one get the mitzvah, the incredible opportunity, to restore sight to someone who has none? I wouldn't trade this privilege for all the money in the world. But I wonder if I might ask one favor..."

He reached into his pocket and carefully

removed a crumpled envelope. It contained, he said, a total of $83... mostly one-dollar bills. "This is what your little girl presented to me as payment for the surgery," he explained quietly. "It represents her savings and what she collected. Do I have your permission to keep it?"

The lump in Sima Rabinowitz's throat was so large that she could do nothing but nod wordlessly.

"You see, Mrs. Rabinowitz," he told her solemnly, "whenever I become discouraged — and we doctors often do, because there are *so many* whom we are unable to help — I reach into my pocket, and my faith, my sense of purpose, is restored; I feel as though your Chavi has paid me *millions*."

"Of course," Sima whispered hoarsely. "Of course..."

At that moment — and for a long time afterwards, whenever she played back the story in her head or shared it with others — Sima Rabinowitz could not see for her tears. At the same time, she knew that her own eyes — indeed, all the eyes in the universe

— had been opened, opened wide, with greater clarity than she ever dreamed possible, to the limitless rewards of *chessed.*

All because of a naïve child who had been silently watching her mother's every move, hanging onto her every word, and following faithfully in each of her footsteps. A child, who, in forging her own path, had illuminated the world.

Heard from: Dr. David Pelcovitz

"Of Course!"

*L*ET US AGREE, for a change, to separate fact from fantasy. For this story, wacky details and amazing events notwithstanding, is all fact.

Life, around Rosh Hashanah time, is about making commitments. The rest of the year, however, is another story. Unless, of course, you are Rabbi Dovid Meisels.

Rabbi Meisels was one of the solitary bastions of chassidic lifestyle and outlook in the wilds of 1970s Chicago. He opened a *shtiebel* and busied himself with the responsibilities typical of Rebbes — and also worked as a *mohel* on the side.

He had learned the ancient practice from his father, who had learned it from *his* father, and he performed it precisely as his ancestors had. More specifically, he had made no adaptations or accommodations to modern times and procedures, and the ritual he performed included *metzitzah b'peh*, suctioning the blood by mouth.

Needless to say, such a practice was deeply frowned upon in germ-conscious America, but this did nothing to deter Rabbi Meisels from performing circumcision the way that he was taught and the way that he revered. Accordingly, his client base in antiseptic, urban Chicago was nominal outside of the Windy City's sparse chassidic population.

But this threatened to change in a really bizarre way the day that Stephanie Silver gave birth to a boy. Dr. Jeffrey Silver, Stephanie's husband, ecstatically called his father, Nate, in upstate New York to apprise him of the long-awaited good news. Nate asked all of the typical questions concerning the delivery and the baby's weight and length, and then posed a question that really threw Jeff for a loop.

"Have you started making arrangements for the bris?"

"Bris? What's a bris?" Jeff wanted to know.

"You know, a circumcision."

"Well, umm, I guess it could be done. I'll check with the hospital and get back to you."

"I am not referring to a hospital procedure. True, circumcision is minor surgery, but it is arranged privately with a *mohel* — a rabbi who performs the ritual."

"Err, I don't know about that. You know that I like things done according to the book and in a sterile environment. I am sure that I can arrange for one of the doctors at the hospital to take care of it."

"Jeffrey, listen to me. A bris is done by a

mohel, and that's all there is to it."

"Where do I find a mole?"

"A mole you find in the ground; for a *mohel* you'll have to check with the Chicago Board of Rabbis, or whatever they have out there. Just ask them for a *mohel*: m-o-h-e-l. I'm sure there are a couple in a city the size of Chicago."

Jeff placed a few calls and ended up with a list of four rabbis — and Dovid Meisels was not one of them. Each *mohel* answered with a flat and resounding "no." Well, actually, the conversation was congratulatory and congenial until he mentioned that the baby was born on Saturday and that he lived in Oak Park.

OAK PARK, ILLINOIS, is home to many Jews, but no religious ones. As such, the neighborhood was devoid of a Torah reading, a *minyan* and numerous other amenities a rabbi would desire on Shabbos.

"What am I supposed to do?" an exasperated Dr. Silver asked *Mohel* Number Four. "You're the fourth rabbi I've asked to circumcise my son on Saturday and also the fourth 'no.'" There was a long silence on the line.

"Well, I have an idea, I guess..." the *mohel* said tentatively. "Though, I imagine it is not exactly what you had in mind..."

"Sock it to me, Rabbi. I didn't have any of this in mind until my father insisted that the baby be circumcised according to Jewish law."

"All right. Rabbi Meisels is a qualified circumciser and I know that as a matter of policy, he will never refuse to perform a circumcision—"

"Did you say Meisels?"

"Yes, Rabbi Dovid Meisels —"

"He wasn't on my list. Are you sure he knows how to do it?"

"I'm quite sure. If he wasn't on the list it's because, err... I mean, it was an oversight. But never mind, just give me a minute and I'll get you his number."

While he waited, Jeffrey pondered the Rabbi's comment: "I don't imagine it is exactly what you had in mind..." A rabbi is a rabbi and a circumciser is a circumciser; what was I supposed to have in mind?

SIMPLY PUT, Rabbi Meisels looked just like a chassidic rebbe and nothing like a medical functionary. He could barely speak English. This much, at least, Jeff should have been able to glean from their initial conversation, but he was so relieved to find a *mohel* who finally agreed to perform the ceremony that he missed this most obvious detail.

"Hello, Rabbi Meisels? This is Dr. Jeffrey Silver and we have a baby boy whom we want circumcised. Can you do it?'

"Of course."

"He was born early Saturday afternoon, and based on my previous phone calls I know to stress that it was a natural delivery. The ceremony will take place in our house in Oak Park. Hello, Rabbi, are you there?"

"Of course."

Jeff couldn't believe it. That last point had been the deal-breaker in all of his previous conversations. "So will you be able to perform the surgery?"

"Of course."

"I am delighted and I shall get back to you later this evening with some logistical details that I hesitated to arrange until I had secured a circumciser. Good-bye, Rabbi."

"Of course, of course."

"That's odd," Jeff mumbled to himself, not exactly sure how to identify just what was so odd about the brief conversation. After his earlier frustration, he was so elated with his success that he called his father right away to inform him of the good news.

WHILE JEFFREY had been unable to pinpoint what was bothering him, Rabbi Meisels did not miss a single nuance. He understood that Dr. Silver had no idea what he was getting himself into, but that when he did, a Jewish child might possibly be deprived of the privilege of entering into the covenant of *Avraham Avinu*. What to do? From Rabbi Meisels' perspective, modifying the components of a bris that Silver and his cronies would find most objectionable was simply not an option.

This was a challenge. The givens: Shabbos, bris procedure, *mohel*'s attire, etc. were not up for discussion. Meisels thought and thought until the good ol' mother of all inventions hatched an idea. It would require, indeed was contingent upon, the assistance of a junior colleague, but the Rabbi was confident that he could bank on his *chavrusa*'s help. As he knew that he had no other option, he also knew that his power of persuasion must be compelling.

RABBI MEISELS turned to his young study partner, Yaakov Homnick, and sincerely requested that he accompany him for Shabbos as his "apprentice/assistant." Rabbi Homnick would lend Rabbi Meisels an appearance of nominal normalcy that was conspicuously absent from his act. In addition to the huge mitzvah involved, Yaakov figured that this was far too wild a trip to miss and he graciously agreed to accompany the Rebbe.

Aside from his yarmulke, Homnick dressed like everyone else and his English vocabulary was infinitely richer than his master's two-word lexis. But most importantly, Rabbi Homnick would provide the pivotal smoke screen at the critical point in the bris.

Rabbi Meisels cared little about how he would appear to the Oak Parkites, but he cared a great deal about pulling off the bris — to the very last detail — in accordance with his tradition. And this is where Homnick would step in. There was, however, one inherent weakness in the game plan.

The strategy that Rabbi Meisels had concocted was contingent upon Rabbi Homnick's serving as the *sandek* — the one who holds the baby on his lap during the actual circumcision. Between the two of them, with some fancy footwork and deft *tallis* draping, they would be able to block key components of the ceremony from view.

The problem was that the grandfather from New York would be attending, and like most grandfathers, he would probably being hoping and expecting to be the *sandek*. They had no chance of finagling his cooperation with their plan.

Rabbis Meisels and Homnick did not know what they were up against. Maybe the grandfather was only traditional and not familiar enough to insist upon the honor; then again, he was traveling all the way from New York and would no doubt want more than a photo op after the ceremony.

Allowing themselves a small prevarication, Meisels and Homnick planned to inform the family that the *sandek* holds the baby only *after* the circumcision. If they would be challenged by a more Jewishly literate attendee, they would concede that some religious fanatics believe that the *sandek* should hold the baby throughout the entire procedure, but that was not the prevalent tradition in Oak Park. Meisels and Homnick were willing to state that as unequivocal fact.

Once Homnick was corralled into the act, he handled all of the arranging, including coordinating a Friday afternoon pick-up by Silver to bring Meisels and Homnick to Oak Park. They were to stay at a Holiday

Inn about seven miles away from the Silver residence where the bris would take place on Saturday at noon.

Aside from the *sandek* ruse, Meisels and Homnick worked out other contingencies, so that they would be fully ready for any eventuality. But none of their conjectures, rehearsals or "creative *halachos*" could have prepared them for their encounter with Jeffrey Silver. He arrived in a sub-compact sports car that was never designed for someone of Rabbi Meisels' dimensions. Contorting himself to fit into the car was an inelegant way to initiate what was never more than an awkward relationship.

Meisels and Homnick had assumed that Silver would be a young, inexperienced father who would readily conform to their instructions. After all, they were the Judaism and circumcision experts. To say that they had underestimated Jeffrey would be putting it charitably.

Silver was, indeed, an inexperienced father, but young he was not. The man was in his mid-forties and after grappling with infertility for over a decade, he was more strung up than the rubber bands in a golf ball. But that was the minor issue.

The major issue — which Jeffrey did not waste any time revealing even before Rabbi Meisels was halfway ensphered into his seat — was that Dr. Silver was an infectious disease specialist. Meisels and Homnick fixed each other with steely, speculative glances and raised their eyebrows. "This is going to be a trippier trip than I had imagined," Yaakov Homnick thought to himself.

"I shall be watching *everything* you do, for in my field, I have seen far too many things go wrong and the consequences can be catastrophic. To be honest, my fear of infection is paranoiac. Molysmophobia is my middle name."

"Of course," Rabbi Meisels interjected, fully inappropriately.

"*Of course*, we don't mean to pry," Yaakov cut in, trying to save his partner's malapropism, "but paranoia is not usually considered an asset in the medical field..."

"There is no amount of precaution that

will suffice to allay my fear of infection," the good doctor went on as if he hadn't been interrupted. "Fear is the great motivator, and skill is its progeny. If necessity is the mother of invention, fear is the mother of competence."

"Of course," Rabbi Meisels commented, remarkably not-inappropriately.

With Homnick translating into rapid-fire Yiddish out of the corner of his mouth, the Rebbe immediately realized that their problems had doubled. Until now, they had assumed that their only problem would be the *metzitzah b'peh*; they had not been concerned about the *priah* — tucking back the foreskin with the thumbnail. It is a split-second procedure, but even a nano-second would be too long for an infection specialist who planned to scrutinize every detail. If Silver were to see this he would pull the plug mid-bris. He claimed that he had observed several circumcisions — pro-phylactic, antiseptic, autoclaved, hospital-sterile-standard surgeries — and if not for his father's insistence, this one would be of the same genre.

Though Silver's late-model sports car glided smoothly along the road, for *mohel* and assistant, the ride was getting bumpier by the minute as Silver sprung more and more surprises, turning their undertaking into Mission Impossible/Obsession Reprehensible. Jeffrey regaled his captive (literally!) audience with a lengthy list of his colleagues from the Infectious Disease Department who would be present, along with other fellow physicians who had performed their share of circumcisions but were curious to observe the Rabbi's technique.

Dr. Jeff then drifted back from the theoretical to the practical. "I insist that the surgical field be pre-coated with Betadine."

"You know what Betadine is, don't you?" Jeffrey inquired.

"Of course," Rabbi Meisels replied with his typical assurance.

Silver wasn't fully convinced, so with little prompting, he began reciting by heart from the pharmaceutical journal. "Betadine Solution contains 10 percent povidone-iodine and is a topical iodophor microbicide...

"Of course," Rabbi Meisels commented.

The remark gave Jeffrey pause but for a moment before he resumed his description of his beloved Betadine. "Povidone-Iodine is a broad-spectrum microbicide with the chemical name of 1-Vinyl-2-pyrrolidinone polymers iodine complex."

Silver was definitely on a roll. From the way he was speaking you would imagine that not only would Betadine stop infection, it could also kill a herd of water buffalo. Though Rabbi Meisels failed to feign interest, understand what was being said or care in the slightest, he did manage to emit another ill-timed, "Of course," making Homnick cringe.

Oblivious to the ubiquitous non sequitur, Silver continued unspooling Betadineology, leading Homnick to wonder if the doctor was so far gone that he thought others actually knew and cared about his subject. Although his recitation was not yet complete (one had to wonder if it ever would be), Dr. Silver interrupted himself to ask, "What do you normally prefer to work with — solution or swab sticks?"

"Of course," Rabbi Meisels answered, exhausting his English vocabulary once again.

"Let me handle this," Homnick hissed in Yiddish. "That's what you brought me along for!"

"Of course?" Silver repeated rhetorically. "How could a choice between a solution and a swab stick be 'of course'?"

"Of course!" Rabbi Meisels parroted, as Homnick began yanking at his hair in frustration.

"Hmm," Silver pondered, but his love of infection-busters rendered him blind to logic. And then, as if he had finally discovered genuine Betadine-enthusiasts, he continued to drone on, "In your profession I'm sure your clients frequently inquire about this antiseptic."

"Of course," Meisels said, coherent, for once, by chance and not design.

"Would you like me to chart out the structural formula for you?"

Anticipating Meisels' inevitable reply, Yaakov quickly jabbed him into silence.

"Okay, if you are not interested in an illustration, I'll continue with the fundamental information everyone wants to know: "The sterile, dark-brown solution is stabilized by glycerin. Inactive Ingredients: ammonium nonoxynol-4 sulfate, nonoxynol-9, purified water, and sodium hydroxide."

"Don't say it!" Rabbi Homnick wanted to scream, but he was too late.

"Of course, of course, of course," Rabbi Meisels said with conviction implying, "Of course to the glycerin, of course to the sodium hydroxide, and of course to the unspoken question, 'What else would you want to discuss when you have total strangers in your car?'"

Somehow, the description of Betadine managed to get them all the way to Oak Park and the circumciser and his assistant were let off at the Holiday Inn.

ON SHABBOS MORNING, the two Rabbis set out to battle a fierce winter storm, shivering more from anticipation of the challenge that lay at their destination than from the frigid weather. Trudging through snow and slipping on ice, the inclement weather seemed to be just one more omen of looming disaster. They clung desperately to the small shred of comfort provided by the knowledge that matters could not possibly get worse. But, true to Murphy's Law, they did.

The stereo was playing in the living room, several doctors were in the den, huddled around the television set watching a Chicago Bears pre-game show and the kettle was whistling merrily in the kitchen. *Prima facie*, the special Shabbos component was missing. But the otherwise joyous atmosphere turned somber when Jeffrey emerged, rather pale, and announced that his wife had contracted Bell's Palsy.

This got the medical contingent buzzing and the non-medical delegation very curious. What both camps had in common was that the strangeness of Stephanie Silver's sudden facial paralysis had made everyone phobic. The whole atmosphere in the house was one of extreme caution — and then, in marched the snow-covered Rabbis Meisels and Homnick.

The fear of Bell's Palsy quickly receded as everyone beheld the bearded, *payos*ed, *shtreimel*ed, white-knickered-to-the-calf, red-nosed Rabbi Dovid Meisels. The fact that his *payos* were frozen at obtuse angles gave him an additional — and unhelpful — martian-like appearance. A hush fell over the room and even the announcer in the background was clicked off in the middle of a salient monologue about the legendary running back, Walter Payton, a.k.a. Sweetness.

Yaakov Homnick, who, in the car, had gracefully slipped into his role as conversationalist, translator and overall PR man, was suddenly gripped by incipient vertigo. He had come along and braved seven miles of snow and wind to experience the intrigue, to observe the clash of cultures, but most importantly, to do a favor and fulfill a Torah commandment. It suddenly hit him with dreadful clarity that they were cruising, nay, speeding towards a disaster far beyond the guaranteed protests and likely desecration of the Almighty's Name.

He played out several scenarios is his mind, each one more catastrophic than the next. He imagined the two of them slapped with lawsuits even before the ceremony had been completed, both of them arrested as medical imposters and handed a seven-digit malpractice grievance. He became woozy as he envisioned ambulances and police squad cars converging on a Shabbos *bris milah*. The news would surely reach their own community, or even be splashed all over the front pages of the Chicago newspapers, and would not enhance their popularity ratings.

Yaakov Homnick is a levelheaded person, but he was suddenly struck by severe panic. He did not seem to be holding up very well and one of the doctors asked him if he was all right. Homnick stammered in a failed attempt to answer the question gracefully. He needn't have worried —

Meisels, never at a loss for (two) words, covered for him with his ever-ready, "Of course."

Homnick tried to think fast and his thoughts were tinged with a sober dose of reality. True, Rabbi Meisels' allegiance to the traditional way of performing *bris milah* was very admirable, and his commitment never to refuse the mitzvah — even if it meant doing it *gratis* — was most commendable, but... in view of this ultra-nervous doctor, who was mega-nervous in spades around anything that could cause an infection — coupled with an environment of curious medical practitioners who wished to observe every aspect of the "rabbinic technique of circumcision," a bit of prudence was indicated. His heart thumped against his rib cage in fear that their intransigence over custom and tradition would set *bris milah* back fifty years in America, God forbid, not to mention land them behind bars, or at least, in debtor's prison.

But good ol' Rabbi Meisels could not be budged. This is the way it was done, he insisted, and this is the way he was taught, and this is the way it will be performed. Period. Yaakov Homnick possessed neither the sangfroid, the toughness, nor the resolve of his mentor and his every nerve leaped and shuddered.

Meanwhile, cars bearing medical professionals of one specialty or another continued to arrive for the procedure. The docs marched in with cheery, "Good afternoons" and "Hellos" but as soon as they saw what their slack-jawed colleagues were gaping at, they, too, were struck with sphinx-like silence. The place looked like a mausoleum on a slow day.

Slowly, Rabbi Homnick began to regain some of his color and rise to the occasion. Just in the clutch, he found his voice and formed a defensive wall between some of the less-timid guests and the master surgeon. Those who actually broke through and attempted to converse with Rabbi Meisels were rewarded with his entire vocabulary, of course.

Dr. Silver was nowhere to be found and it was assumed that he was either tending to his baby, helping his wife or looking after the Betadine. In his absence, the grandfather, hailing from Schenectady, New York, began making introductions and shaking hands. He met Rabbi Meisels, of course, and informed the circumciser that he wished to be the "*Zon Dock.*"

"Of course, of course," Rabbi Meisels beamed. He saw his first break and he jumped at it, marshaling a rush of English for the occasion. "You vill be zee *Zon Dock.* Isn't zat right, Rabbi Homnick?"

"Of course," Rabbi Homnick said for a change, picking up the lead. "Are you familiar with all of the duties and religious obligations incumbent upon the *Zon Dock*?" he pressed the unsuspecting grandfather.

"Umm, eh, err, well..."

At that moment, Rabbi Meisels knew that he could not have picked a better assistant. Homnick rattled on about the supreme honor and lofty merit of being a *Zon Dock*, contingent, of course, upon carefully heeding and never straying — even for an instant — from the instructions the surgical team would provide.

Nate Silver stood ramrod straight and the earth, frankly, did not move as he waited for the instructions to be conferred upon him. "You must prepare yourself a seat exactly ten feet away from us..." Homnick had a thought, but considering the gravity of the issue and how far out of his league it was, he turned to Rabbi Meisels and in the most respectful and obsequious tone implored, "Rebbe, would it be kosher if Mr. Silver were to sit eleven or even twelve feet away?"

Rabbi Meisels had to ponder this weighty question for a moment and began to stroke his beard as he paced a few steps. Consternation gripped his face. Finally, he raised his head, looking as if he had just had an apotheosis of a kind.

"Of course."

Thus spaketh the religious authority and Nate Silver began measuring the exact distance from the point that Rabbi Homnick indicated.

"Mr. Silver," Yaakov called after him, "as soon as we have completed the circumcision, we will hand you the baby. You, and you *alone*, must embrace your grandson until the blessing ceremony concludes. Therefore, if someone offers to assist or relieve you, you *must* decline. The *Zon Dock* may not let go of the baby for even a second!"

Homnick peered up at Rabbi Meisels to verify that he had quoted the law accurately. The elderly Rabbi nodded his head solemnly, adding senior rabbinic weight and authority to the directions just detailed and implying in no uncertain terms, "the law is the law."

Homnick was on a roll and was even beginning to enjoy himself. He decided to milk the opportunity for even more strategic gain. "Customarily, the *Zon Dock* selects several important people to flank him on his right and left as it adds more dignity and solemnity to the ceremony." Meisels nodded most vigorously. Simultaneously, as if they had rehearsed this part a hundred times, Meisels and Homnick began to escort some of the most inquisitive and talkative doctors towards the *Zon Dock* docking area.

Dr. Silver came downstairs and noticed that the show was getting on the road without him. He quickly informed the circumcisers that his brother-in-law, Sumner, Stephanie's brother, would be the "godfather." Meisels looked at Homnick uncomprehendingly.

Yaakov didn't miss a beat. "The godfather," the surgeon's assistant declared, "must hand the baby from the circumciser to the *Zon Dock* directly *after* the ceremony. But as I'm sure you know," he said, buoyed by Jeff's vacant expression, "it is critical that the godfather sit adjacent to the *Zon Dock* during the surgery."

Once again, Homnick wished to check his facts with the master so he looked to Rabbi Meisels for approval. The two nodded to each other like consulting surgeons.

Everyone in the room, besides the surgical team and Nate, was a doctor. The only other exception was Sumner, the godfather, who was still in medical school. And whereas Jeffrey was nervous, Sumner was hyper-nervous-on-steroids. It was rather remarkable that such an anxious individual would wish to pursue a career of medicine, and even more remarkable that a person allergic to blood had managed to make it so far through medical school.

Sumner was not present at the moment for he was keeping his sister company. Stephanie was embarrassed to appear in public with the ravages of Bell's Palsy on her face.

The last of the doctors pulled up and they hastened to hang up their coats as they saw that the service was about to commence. But the new docs, instead of positioning themselves near the distant island of *Zon Dock* and the phalanx of guests that Meisels and Homnick had carefully choreographed precisely ten feet away, moved right in to ground zero. And then the questions began to fly fast and furious.

"Will you be using the Plastibell method?" one of the doctors wanted to know.

"Of course," Rabbi Meisels responded.

"I thought almost everyone," interjected a second, "uses the Gomco clamp."

"Of course," agreed the circumciser.

"Do you mean to say," asked yet a third, "that you will not be employing the Tara clamp?

Predictably, Rabbi Meisels said — yes, you guessed it. Homnick was finding it exceedingly difficult to cover for his partner and the situation was rapidly spinning out of control.

"Let me get this straight," inquired a different specialist, a look of incredulity plastered on his face, "you favor all of these methods over the Sheldon Clamp?"

Before Rabbi Meisels could offer his standard response, yet another doctor interpolated, "In our hospital we used to use the Ross circumcision ring, but I know that in West Suburban they use the Yellen clamp. Isn't that right, George?"

"In Children's Memorial and in Saint Joe's they use the Tara clamp," an inchoate voice echoed from deep in the room.

"Well at Mercy and Rush Oak Park I've

only seen them use the Ross circumcision ring," some doctor asserted emphatically.

"Why," one physician said, his voice rising above all of the others, "don't we ask the, er, surgeon what he intends to do?" Suddenly the room quieted down and all eyes focused on Rabbi Meisels.

For once, the Rabbi intuited that "of course" would not be a beneficial response. In complete exasperation he muttered, *"Vuss ken ich machen?"*

"Machen?" one of the most senior doctors, actually clad in a lab coat, repeated, utterly confounded. "I thought it was pronounced *Magen.*"

Yaakov fired his partner a thumbs up. The senior doctor then stated sonorously, "Don't you gentlemen know that all Jewish circumcisers employ the Magen clamp unless they use a scalpel by the freehand method?"

Homnick resumed breathing. He realized that he would have been amused had he not felt so absolutely apprehensive about what would happen next. Things were looking glum and high noon had come and passed.

EVERYBODY WAS milling around, consulting their watches and waiting for Sumner-the-godfather to come downstairs. Little did they know that more than keeping Stephanie company, he was trying to muster the nerve to be present at the surgery.

Finally, they heard the door open upstairs, followed by the patter of feet, at which point Jeffrey informed all those present that it was time to apply his beloved Betadine, which he proceeded to do. He then announced with arms outstretched like an evangelical preacher at a revival, "Air Dry, Air Dry!" And for two minutes, the baby squirmed and screamed with an open diaper, displaying for all to see, the brown, Betadine-stained surgical objective.

Just then jumpy, edgy, how-in-the-world-did-medical-school-accept-him Sumner arrived on the scene. He took one look at the surgical field, confused the Betadine for blood, and summarily fainted right into the huddle of doctors congregated around Jeffrey.

It was a total knockout, a perfect strike. Meisels looked at Homnick, Homnick looked at Meisels, and in a flash they knew that Opportunity was bellowing from the rooftops. "Now!" Homnick hissed, and in a flash, Meisels and Homnick executed the ol' Notre Dame switch. Rabbi Meisels put his back to the wounded, felled by Sumner, while Homnick grabbed a chair facing the master surgeon, threw his *tallis* high in the air over the two of them and accepted the hand-off of the baby from Meisels.

Meanwhile, the *Zon Dock* and those in his entourage who were unaffected when Sumner saw red, remained glued to their places precisely as they had been instructed. But all was not quiet on the medical front. Jeffrey was caught in a medical, ethical and paternal dilemma. His son was undergoing surgery within arm's reach, but not before his eyes. His brother-in-law-cum-godfather had collapsed in his lap. He couldn't miss the surgery, but what was he to do with Sumner — especially with all of his Hippocratically-oathed colleagues looking on?

Meisels had set the metal guard of one-of-the-above varieties in place and made the cut. Just as he was about to exercise his thumbnail to perform the *priah*, Dr. Silver was back with Sumner, rather the worse for the wear, unsteadily supported at his side. Sumner's left arm was draped over Jeffrey's shoulder and his right arm was draped over Jeffrey's colleague's neck. Silver removed the *tallis* at a critical moment and where Sumner had seen red, Jeffrey saw infection!

Providentially, at that very second, Sumner came to. This time seeing real blood, he collapsed backward, taking down with him, like a human domino, everyone who wasn't in the *Zon Dock* position. They landed between two tall, ornate wicker chairs. Fortunately they were not harmed by the furniture, but they were effectively buried and hopelessly intertwined between the chairs and each other. Everyone but the surgeon and his assistant had been diverted. Meisels expeditiously performed the *metzitzah b'peh* and then took all the time in the world finishing up so that Jeffrey could observe and approve.

RABBI DOVID MEISELS performed the bris the way his father had instructed him without a single witness noticing anything afoul. All they saw was the Before and After.

Yaakov Homnick found himself in a near-Sumner state, but not because of the blood. He had envisioned the worst and realized a major miracle was needed. And a major miracle is precisely what they got; it could not be written off any other way.

Rabbi Meisels, the utterly, indeed impossibly, sincere individual who steadfastly wished to honor his commitment, was provided with the necessary Heavenly intervention to enable him to do so.

And as to whether there is a lesson to be gleaned about upholding an earnest commitment, the answer is a resounding, "Of course!"

Heard from: Yaakov Homnick

Faithful

Helpful Lyrics

*H*E WAS HAILED as the most embracing leader in an organization not known for outreach, the most accepting in a group not considered hugely tolerant. Rabbi Moshe Halberstam *zt"l*, danced determinedly to his own tune, a tune with a most holy refrain.

It was: "How, my fellow Jew, can I help you?"

He originated the score, he penned the lyrics, he choreographed each move. The wellspring for Rabbi Halberstam's opus was something beautiful, deep and rare. It was the quality of compassionate listening: Rabbi Halberstam's genius ability to hear, with his heart, words that were not said. Listen...

LATE ONE AFTERNOON, a distraught young man appeared at Rabbi Halberstam's door. Most visitors who walked this well-trodden path came with complex halachic dilemmas. This was not such an instance.

The fellow was a stranger to the Rabbi. It was a Thursday, and the man's wife had just started to experience complications in her pregnancy. "Preparations for Shabbos have just begun..." he said anxiously, concern etched all over his face.

There was no need to elaborate.

In the soft, yet very firm tone that was his trademark, Rabbi Moshe Halberstam proclaimed in the name of the Law that the young man must cancel all of their Shabbos guests, remove his wife from the kitchen, and put her to bed. He was duty-bound to ensure that she had complete rest, and he was absolved from other obligations so that he could fulfill this responsibility. These, declared the Rabbi, were unmistakably the dictates of the Law.

As for the *seudos*, he should purchase Shabbos take-out food and serve his wife in bed. Rabbi Halberstam's decree was direct and to the point: Q & A; dilemma and resolution.

This should have been the end of the story, but as the Rabbi escorted his subdued visitor to the door, he sensed that his instructions would not be obeyed. He was poised to repeat his directives in the plainest of words, when suddenly, he, who could hear what was not spoken, heard and understood all with the loudness of a thunderclap.

Reb Moshe reached inside his pockets to remove every bill he had and pressed them into the hands of the sorrowful stranger. "Have a good and enjoyable Shabbos," he told the startled young man in a soothing voice, "and don't hesitate to buy yourselves the tastiest dishes!"

A pitch higher, a pitch lower, a beat slower or faster; this was the melody that he played, and the refrain was always the same. *"How, my fellow Jew, can I help you?"*

RABBI HALBERSTAM was known as the "young lion" of the *Bada"tz*, though "young" is a relative term when referring to a group of septua-and-octogenarians.

In any case, he felt the wings of time beating at his back and was careful with his minutes, apportioning them wisely and never squandering a single one.

Like many other halachic authorities, Rabbi Halberstam made himself available to the public on a daily basis. There was a fixed period each morning when he would answer queries and render decisions. One could only solicit his sage advice during those carefully circumscribed hours; there were no exceptions.

By allocating these specific times, the rest of his day was available for uninter-rupted Torah study, and the august duties that a *dayan* for the *Bada"tz* shouldered. Creating a schedule and enforcing it was one of Rabbi Moshe Halberstam's secrets of success.

And so, it was most unusual to hear repeated knocks on his door one afternoon, nearly two hours after his busy "walk-in" hours had drawn to a close.

Always one to give others the benefit of the doubt, Reb Moshe glanced repeatedly at his watch, but even the Champion of Judging Favorably would have found this one a tough call. Assured that his watch showed the correct time, Rabbi Halberstam and his study partner continued to learn — or at least, they *attempted* to learn. The continuous knocking was beginning to sound like the thunder of war and it was only growing more insistent.

Eventually, Rabbi Halberstam shrugged his shoulders in resignation. His study partner arose and gently lifted one of the ribs of the *tris* — that nifty Israeli window-blind that totally blocks out the light. Peering through the crack, he caught a glimpse of the perpetrators who pointedly chose to ignore the posted hours, and reported back to the Rabbi.

"Let them in," Reb Moshe sighed, gesturing with a wave of his hand, and a middle-aged woman entered, accompanied by an adolescent girl. If the woman had any misgivings about disturbing the Rabbi during "off hours" they weren't readily apparent. The girl, however, stood there listlessly, without affect, shoulders slumped.

"Honorable Rabbi," the woman began, "this is Malka Sternfeld, and I am her teacher..."

The conversation commenced in Yiddish and it was apparent from Malka's attire and braids that she was a student in one of the chassidic girls' schools in the vicinity. "Malka," the teacher continued, "has just gotten up from sitting *shiva* for her mother..."

Rabbi Halberstam's eyes narrowed when he heard this, and he immediately asked to hear the last name again.

"Sternfeld," the teacher repeated, uncertainly.

"*Aiyy!*" he groaned, vigorously shaking

his head from side to side. *"Oy, what a tzad-dekes!"* he intoned, repeating the same words in a heartfelt dirge.

The Rabbi's moans caused a slight smile to form on Malka's downturned lips and a bit of light to flash from her guarded eyes. But Rabbi Halberstam continued to wear the face of sadness as he murmured a host of superlatives regarding the deceased; his brow appeared furrowed in memories.

"Rabbi, if you don't mind..." the teacher said hesitantly, unsure if she should interrupt his reveries, "Malka wishes to know... if she should sing in the upcoming school performance, in which she has a leading role. A musical..."

Reb Moshe cut her off in mid-sentence. "I understand what you are concerned about, and I wish to make things very clear. You probably believe that it is inappropriate to sing in public during the period of mourning; you may also insist that your heart will not be in it.

"But there is a crucial factor that cannot be dismissed, ladies. The proceeds from this production, I assume, will be going to charity. I *also* assume that you, Malka'la, are the star who will be drawing in considerable revenues. In other words, since your singing will be benefiting so many poor, downtrodden souls, I do not know of a *hetter* that would rightly *absolve* you from performing! And raising all of this money for needy people would be a tremendous merit, honoring your mother of blessed memory."

Another classic ruling for Rabbi Halberstam, expert listener to words unsaid, who could hear the music, no matter how muted, inside each soul. The effect was immediate. As the Rabbi elucidated his *psak,* Malka's entire body language changed; she blossomed before his very eyes. Her mother's life had, tragically, ended — but at that moment, her *own* life had been returned to her.

Teacher and student had turned to leave, when Rabbi Halberstam asked Malka if she could do him a "huge" favor.

"Could I?" responded the invigorated youngster, as if her greatest wish had been granted.

"Would you mind returning with two tickets for your production — one for the *Rebbetzin* and one for our daughter? I know how much they would *love* to attend your performance..."

The *Dayan* then removed some money from his pocket. "Please," the teacher protested, "please, Rabbi, *Dayan*... it would be an honor for us to give you complimentary tickets!"

"I won't hear of it," the Rabbi demurred. "The proceeds are for *tzedakah*, so please, please, do not deprive me of this mitzvah!"

Rabbi Moshe Halberstam saw them out, locked the door, readjusted the *tris,* and briskly sat down to resume his learning.

His young study-partner stared at him, dumbfounded, struggling to absorb what had just transpired. He had no doubt that his distinguished mentor, the noted *Bada"tz Dayan,* had ample basis for his unconventional halachic ruling. His only question was this: Did Reb Moshe *really* know who the deceased was, and was he truly privy to the many facets of her character?

All it took was one look at the twinkle in the Rabbi's eyes, to know the truth. "*Nu!*" Rabbi Halberstam pressed on, forever conscious of time. "Let us continue!"

Heard from: Rabbis Yehudah Kohn and Eli Meir Klugman

The Story Worth a Million

*T*HERE WERE but a few stairs leading up to Rabbi Erez Mishkofsky's Jerusalem apartment. For his former student, Dovi — ringing the buzzer expectantly and with a full heart — the road to this doorstep, to this momentous day, had been quite long and complicated.

The backstory was all too familiar: good boy, good family, good yeshivah — but something fundamental was amiss. Dovi probably started slipping through the cracks during elementary school, and by the time he got to high school he was almost fully submerged. Miraculously, he managed to graduate, whereupon he bade the yeshivah world a final goodbye and shut the door. Tightly.

Rabbi Erez Mishkofsky's mission in life was to foil the best-laid plans of disaffected youths like Dovi. He opened a yeshivah — pointedly never referred to as a "yeshivah" — that focused on finding employment for its students, and disguised any actual learning with all sorts of clever gimmicks designed to keep the restless *bachurim* in the fold.

Dovi's own path back was by way of Chabad. He, himself, was at a loss to explain it, for he had never been exposed to anything Lubavitch at home or in school. Notwithstanding, Chabad quickly became the anchor to Judaism that had always eluded him.

And so, bearing many lessons and many blessings from his erstwhile mentor, Dovi left Rabbi Mishkofsky's orbit, and entered a different one. He was aware that it was Rabbi Mishkofsky who had facilitated the journey that had taken him to Chabad's doorstep.

There was nothing half-hearted about Dovi's embrace of his new life. Not surprisingly, he soon became engaged to a lovely young woman who shared his fervent convictions. When their wedding invitations came back from the printer, Dovi was most eager to honor Rabbi Mishkofsky in the Jerusalem tradition, by delivering his in person.

And now, creamy white envelope in hand, he waited impatiently for the Rabbi or his gracious wife of many years, Chani, to answer the doorbell. He knew (though modesty and piety would prevent him from ever dwelling or remarking on this fact) that he was one of Rabbi Mishkofsky's success stories. But he could not know — yet — that this story was one of a series of miracles transcending time and space that would ultimately converge at a single point.

THE *ROSH YESHIVAH* was delighted to see his former student and overjoyed by his momentous news. Touched by Dovi's thoughtful gesture, he keenly examined the handsome invitation. And then, slowly, one eyebrow crept upward. "Your *kallah*," the Rabbi asked haltingly. "She's from a Lubavitch family?"

Dovi nodded affirmatively.

"Might you know the last time that your mother-in-law-to-be went to the Rebbe for a dollar?" Rabbi Mishkofsky referred to the Lubavitcher Rebbe's custom of personally distributing dollar bills to long lines of admirers who were then tasked with donating the money to charity. In Lubavitch circles, a dollar that the Rebbe himself had handled was considered to be blessed; no chassid would dream of giving it away. Instead, they would substitute a different bill to fulfill the mitzvah of alms to the poor.

Those fortunate enough to have received one of the Rebbe's dollars would either carry this talisman at all times, display it prominently in their homes or businesses or tuck it lovingly away for safekeeping. No matter how far they might live from Chabad's Brooklyn headquarters, the

Rebbe's followers would faithfully undertake the pilgrimage to be personally in his presence and participate in this Lubavitch rite. Outsiders, by and large, were either unaware of the custom or paid it scant attention.

This was why it was so odd for a decidedly non-chassidic, Lithuanian rabbi like Erez Mishkofsky to pose such a question. Nonetheless, Dovi pledged that he would soon return with the answer.

Two *Shabbosos* hence, Dovi was invited to be the guest of his future in-laws, and immediately upon his arrival, he posed the Rabbi's query to the lady of the house. "Shevat, 5751," his mother-in-law replied at once with the assurance of a baseball fan spewing stats at Cooperstown — without missing a beat from her last-minute Shabbos preps or averting her eye from the clock.

He meant to ask her to elaborate for him in greater detail at a more opportune moment, but he forgot. So taken was he by the light that shined from the eyes of his Tirza, by the warmth of Shabbos in this happy household, by the new family that welcomed him with open arms...

DOVI DUTIFULLY returned to Rabbi Mishkofsky to report on the provenance of his future mother-in-law's dollar. When he repeated the date, "*Shevat*, 5751," the Rabbi's eyes suddenly assumed a faraway look, and for what seemed like several minutes, he retreated into silence. When he finally spoke, his words crackled with the energy and sly provocation that Dovi remembered so well from the classroom.

He had, the Rabbi told Dovi, an offer to make him. But the offer, he emphasized, would not come cheaply. In fact, his precise words were: "I have a story for you that is worth a million dollars — but I'll tell it to you for $10,000."

Even the discounted price was a tad steep, so Dovi and the Rabbi playfully entered into negotiations. After some haggling, they agreed upon a barter that suited them both. In dollars and cents, this meant that Rabbi Mishkofsky agreed to reveal his ten-grand tale gratis in exchange for an invitation to a *sheva brachos* at which both families would be present. They solemnly shook on the deal.

The wedding took place *b'sha'a tova umutzlachas*, and the very last *sheva brachos* was held in *Gan Sacher*, Jerusalem's largest park, where the groom's uncle, a local caterer of renown, set up a barbecue. It was a casual but joyful event that would conclude the week of wedding festivities and transform Tirza and Dovi from bride and groom into husband and wife.

It was an honor to have a scholar of Rabbi Mishkofsky's stature grace the *simcha*, but along with the joy, a sense of mystery and anticipation — even anxiety — hung in the air. Word had spread of Dovi's "negotiation" with the Rabbi, and everyone felt himself in the presence of something... momentous. It was apparent that his message would go beyond the usual fare of praise for the families and a charge to the young couple. Indeed, all of the distinguished speakers leading up to Erez Mishkofsky had the feeling that they were merely a mediocre warm-up act for the grand finale.

Thus, as he slowly rose to his feet, the lively celebrants immediately fell into hushed silence. The electricity was palpable — no one had ever been in the presence of a million-dollar story before!

Rabbi Mishkofsky slowly scanned the outdoor assemblage; he certainly did not have to wait for silence.

"From the time of my wedding, I learned in a yeshivah in Netanya," he began in a quiet, somber voice, selecting his words with great care. "I was part of the *kollel*, and a number of us were very involved with the *bachurim*. Something had gone terribly awry with some of the boys in our yeshivah, and factually, I knew that we did not have a monopoly on errant youth.

"Boys who were once deeply immersed in their learning, who once conducted themselves as Torah students should, were becoming completely disaffected. Something was luring them outside the yeshivah walls; it was permeating their minds and hearts, and contaminating their souls. Everyone recognized the negative effect these boys were having upon the yeshivah and it had become a source of great consternation.

"But all the focus seemed to be on *how these boys were ruining the yeshivah*... no one was talking about the sorry state of these boys' *Yiddishe neshomos*!"

Rabbi Mishkofsky's voice shook and his shoulders sagged as he summoned up the heavy burden of his anguish and frustration. "I *tried* to direct the administration's attention to what was being ignored... I tried! But they had never experienced defections of such magnitude before and clearly did not know how to proceed. So they averted their eyes from the spiritual welfare of these boys, and decided to concentrate their limited resources where they would be most likely to bear fruit...

"I was tormented by this. My learning suffered, I couldn't sleep; I felt compelled to do something, but I didn't know what. All I *did* know was that we were on the brink of a disaster. Keeping these troubled boys in the confines of the yeshivah was untenable for them, and — especially as their ranks swelled — a serious liability to the others.

But expelling them to the streets would be unconscionable, because all that anchored them, all that prevented them from washing out to sea entirely, was their tenuous connection with the yeshivah.

"I came upon an interim solution of renting them a house in Pardes Katz. This would distance them from the yeshivah, yet enable us to keep them in a monitored environment.

"And I," said the Rabbi wryly, "was to be the monitor.

"I knew it wouldn't be a perfect solution, and about this I was one-hundred-percent correct. The boys could not be left to their own devices, but any attempt to channel their behavior would cause them to bolt. And what about *davening*, learning, meals, rent? The whole thing was an administrative nightmare and a psychological quagmire... and it all fell upon my narrow shoulders.

"I was never trained for the mission at hand, and had to compensate for my inexperience with all the love that I possessed

— and most importantly, with a massive investment of my time. Time, I quickly discovered, was the most powerful weapon in my limited arsenal. These boys needed constant infusions of empathy, concern and friendship in order to gain their trust. But these curatives had to be administered carefully, slowly, patiently... over time. Indeed, had the boys received the precious gift of *someone's time* at an earlier juncture, perhaps their struggles would not have metastasized into such an all-out crisis situation...

"But time, alas, is the most difficult commodity to marshal; and I surely had no more of it to spare than the official heads of the yeshivah. However, this 'satellite school' was *my* vision, and it was incumbent upon me to see it through. I was prepared to sacrifice *everything* for it — everything! At least, I *thought* I was..."

Rabbi Mishkofsky took a deep breath and surveyed his rapt audience.

"At *s'machos* like this one, we shower the happy couple with wishes for their future, and we speak of the joy and holiness of building a *bayis ne'eman b'Yisrael.* It is not easy for me to speak frankly about some of the struggles — my own struggles — in this process."

Again, he paused, shifting his weight.

"As I said, *I* was resigned to the enormous toll this work would take on my life, my time — but my wife, Chani, felt otherwise. She claimed I had taken on responsibilities that were way over my head, at the expense of my obligations to my family and to my learning. The way she phrased it, with a touch of sarcasm, was that I had been 'demoted' from an *avreich* to a *rosh yeshivah.* A *rosh yeshivah*, she argued, has no time to learn, no time for family and no time for himself. 'I never agreed to marry a *rosh yeshivah*,' she told me, 'and I have not changed my mind.'"

With just one glance, the Rabbi could see that everyone present was experiencing his gut-wrenching dilemma.

"I never doubted for a minute that my dear wife understood how vital my mission was, and that she was only looking out for my best interests. Nonetheless, I countered that the work I was engaged in was *pikuach nefesh*, and no argument could take precedence. But Chani was hardly convinced, and insisted that I was violating our nuptial understanding.

"She had her view, and I had mine, and a chasm grew between us. The disagreement did not wane over time. I believed in what I was doing, but I knew, at the same time, that I was jeopardizing my *shalom bayis*. Yet I still did nothing about it. I don't know what I was expecting — wait, I take that back, I *do* know: I was expecting her to get used to the status quo. But this was not to be.

"After one particularly heated argument, we both finally understood that our home was resting upon a volcano, one that could unleash its molten lava at any moment, engulfing everything around it for miles. One way or another, this issue had to be resolved.

"We decided to go for a long drive and not return until we had achieved a meeting of the minds. But what was left to say about nis issue, when we had already said everything a thousand times? We were long past the point of discussion. We were searching for a sign — some indication, an omen of some sort — that would show us what to do.

"We had driven as far north as *Park Ha'Yarden* when we decided to stop for a picnic lunch. We sat ourselves down on the grass, just a few feet from a restful natural pool into which streamed a waterfall. I sat facing the water, while Chani had her back to it. And there we both ate in silence, wondering — doubting, really — whether this rift could ever be healed.

"Suddenly I spotted something red tumbling down the falls. Was it a red bundle, a satchel of some sort, or... *were my eyes deceiving me*? I immediately leapt to my feet and jumped into the water — suit, shoes and all. The bundle's first bob to the surface was, miraculously, fully within my grasp. It was a little girl, no more than a toddler. In my arms she was flailing, gasping, coughing and spitting out water — thank God, very much alive."

At this point there was an audible gasp from the audience, and the mother of the bride turned ashen. Rabbi Mishkofsky forged on.

"I staggered out of the water, gripping the 'bundle' and very shaken. The child was terrified, of course, but Chani quickly wrapped her up in our picnic blanket, and after a few pats on the back, she seemed almost back to normal, which is more than I could say for the two of *us*!

"The whole thing happened in the blink of an eye — so quickly, we realized, that the child's family might not even know yet that she had gone missing. So Chani and I immediately began the trek to the upper terrace of the park — not an easy one, in my sopping-wet state, carrying a squirming, drenched child in my arms...

"When we got there, we immediately saw a large family spread out across a number of blankets with lots of children, grandparents too, I think... they were eating and talking and laughing and enjoying themselves, and clearly had no inkling that the little girl in red was *not* happily ensconced among her boisterous siblings and cousins.

"As I approached them, I did not have to say a word. Everyone stared at me in horror, transfixed, and unable, at first, to move. The child's mother became hysterical as she grasped the enormity of what had occurred, and the unspeakable tragedy of what had *almost* occurred.

She began shrieking, and a torrent of words rushed from her mouth, all equally incoherent. She pulled the child from my arms and held her and hugged her and kissed her. Gradually, her words became more comprehensible and she repeatedly thanked God, myself, my wife..."

At this point, the exuberant crowd that had gathered to toast and celebrate could no longer blink back the tears in their eyes. Erez Mishkofsky's voice rang out over their muffled sobs.

"How can I ever thank you, how can I ever thank you," the child's mother repeated over and over! Suddenly, her tear-drenched eyelids fluttered, and she called for somebody to go fetch her purse. I insisted that I sought no reward for my actions, but the woman was adamant. Gently, she removed a single dollar bill from her wallet and attempted to hand it to me. Lest anyone misconstrue the proffered reward to mean that she valued my act of heroism at approximately four shekel, she quickly explained that this was no ordinary dollar bill.

"She was, in fact, offering me the most precious thing she owned: a dollar given to her by the Lubavitcher Rebbe himself in the month of Shevat, 5751, as she had duly noted on the bill itself.

"I repeated again that I sought no remuneration — that I had simply done what I was supposed to do — and was pleased to be of help. To no avail. I finally had to break it to her that this particular dollar was of negligible meaning to *me*, and given that the Rebbe had passed on, it would be a mistake for her to part with *this* precious heirloom."

As he uttered the word "this," for the most dramatic effect imaginable, Rabbi

Mishkofsky gingerly removed the Rebbe's wrinkled dollar from his coat pocket.

"But friends, what can I tell you? My entreaties were in vain. This was one insistent lady!"

At that point, a wave of tentative laughter broke the crescendo of tension. Even the bride's mother had gotten some of her color back, but her eyes still swam with tears and her smile was punctuated by tiny sobs.

"Now you may think," he continued in a matter-of-fact tone, "that I was the savior of that little girl, our *kallah* of today. But that is not the full story.

"What brought my wife and me to the park that day was a last-ditch attempt to find an answer to our deepest dilemma. Once that baby fell down the waterfall, it became absolutely clear to both of us that I must devote myself to *hatzolah* work. My calling was to save others, and an unmistakable sign had tumbled from the Heavens attesting to this.

"Because of this life-altering moment, we moved our family to Jerusalem where we set up a yeshivah in the suburbs for boys who need a *different* approach. Boys who need more time, more love — and who need our holy Torah *more*, not less, than the more compliant yeshivah student. Today's groom is one of our premiere alumni, and how fitting it is that he has married the individual so responsible for the establishment of the yeshivah."

Rabbi Mishkofsky offered a final blessing to the stunned bride and groom. Afterwards, Dovi fell upon him with a mute embrace. Slowly the Rabbi made his way back to his seat, through an ocean of awed silence. It was easily worth ten grand, this saga of a single dollar.

IT WAS THE bride's emotional mother who broke the spell. Across the long table, she raised a tremulous voice, and all eyes were upon her.

"I must tell you all that the last time I saw him, he was a *skinny* fellow without a beard or *rosh yeshivah* attire." And then, dabbing the corner of her eye with a handkerchief, she added breathlessly, "and he also wasn't *dry*!"... lifting everyone to ringing cheers and laughter, which quickly segued into *Shir Hamaalos*, sung in a lilting wedding melody that could surely be heard through the cities of Judah, the streets of Jerusalem and beyond, straight to the Heavens.

Heard from: Rabbi Michael Hoffman

The Great Divide

*F*OR THOSE who may talk the talk, but are clueless as to the walk, here is a refreshing anecdote. As stories go, it is not amazing, stupefying or otherwise out of the ordinary — but, still, refreshing. It is a tale about the Great Divide in American Jewish life.

And what divide might that be? The reader (that's you) is probably thinking that there is no need to wax melodramatic about differences in outlook, observance and lifestyles, for these are mundane divides. I, however, am referring to the *Great* Divide.

The Great Divide is a geographic anomaly that goes by the name, "Verrazano-Narrows Bridge," and separates New York from the rest of the Union. For the sake of clarity, when the *oilem* says, "New York," it refers neither to New York State nor to New York City; it refers to the Borough of Brooklyn.

True, this may ring a tad august and presumptuous, but Brooklynites cannot be blamed for a phenomenon that is as American as apple pie. America is the land of supermarkets, superstars, Superman, and the Super Bowl. The assumption is that if something is Number One in America it retains that status throughout the world; hence the top American boxer is the World Heavyweight Champion and America's best baseball team wins the World Series. Presumably, people from Brooklyn apply similar reasoning in referring to their borough as New York (or, more precisely, New *Yawk*). The geographic reality is that the Verrazano Bridge does not get you out of the state; it does not even get you out of New York City, but it *does* get you "Out of Town"! If you have lost the logic somewhere en route, you have revealed where you are from, or more precisely, where you are *not* from.

Brooklyn boasts the greatest concentration of Jews — fine, hard-working, generous, devoted individuals — that any city has ever hosted. There is no reason to make light of Brooklyn Jewry's sterling qualities for they are indeed long and detailed, and yet... there is a divide, a great divide between Jews who inhabit this borough and all others. When it comes down to it, this difference is characteristic not only of Jews, for people, no matter where they live, are influenced by their environments.

Apparently, living in an urban area with so many millions of people and being exposed to the anguished bedlam of the City — the homeless; the drug addicts; the crowds so dense that people appear to be standing in line just to walk down the sidewalks; the staccato clamor of the jackhammers; the steam pouring upward from the sewers as if the world underneath were an inferno; the tall, ominous visage of buildings; the daily descent into the steely entrails of the asphalt earth to ride the rattling subway system; the stink of exhaust fumes mixed with the stench of at least a thousand fast-food joints — takes its toll. A distanced reserve is created, perhaps even a hardness, almost unheard of in small-town America where most everyone knows everyone else, or at least conducts himself as if he did.

My experience, as one who has spent some of the best years of his life in Kings County (a.k.a. Brooklyn), is that Brooklynites are in no way offended by being referred to as "in-towners" and having the rest of the world referred to as "out-of-towners." It is practically a matter of pride to them and is a label they wear comfortably on their sleeves.

In fact, at the end of a well-attended yeshivah convention in Baltimore in the fall of 2007, the organizers wished to arrange return transportation for the delegates and announced repeatedly that all "out-of-towners" should move to the left side of the auditorium. When participants had finished rearranging themselves, the right side of the auditorium was filled only with Baltimoreans — and Brooklynites!

FEBRUARY, 1997. Josh Stern, Miami

Beach native but currently a resident of Jerusalem, was making one of those lightning trips to America to attend a *simcha* and also get two weeks' worth of business and shopping done in three days. He was on a roll until Wednesday the 12th of February, when New York City awakened to weather cold enough to freeze lava.

The sky over Brooklyn was the color of parchment and on satellite photos it looked like two crocodiles were crawling up the Eastern seaboard. What this meant on the ground was a swirling blizzard of snow that pirouetted and drifted in winds gusting up to 40 miles an hour, creating a wind chill well below zero.

The snows that had begun late Tuesday night continued to fall intermittently, with inch-an-hour bursts in the morning and less as the day waned. A romantic blanket of snow, so pristine and pure that it looked as if it had given birth to the word *white,* concealed the litter on the sidewalks.

Schoolchildren, muffled to the eyes and thrilled by the school closure, frolicked where the snow was fluffy and deep. The remaining New Yorkers were suffering. Airports were useless, highways were treacherous, thousands of homes lost power and countless businesses opened late or not at all. Snow accumulation in Brooklyn was 14.5 inches in Prospect Park, making this storm the biggest in New York City since the two-foot behemoth of December 1993.

The New York City Sanitation Department deployed 1,400 salt spreaders and snowplows to scrape around the clock. Their job was to clear thousands of miles of streets where alternate-side parking and street-cleaning rules were suspended. The mounds of snow molded by plows looked like ruins littering a battlefield, preventing parking on streets already narrowed by snow embankments.

THAT AFTERNOON, Josh was scheduled to meet Malka Hirschfeld, a senior director of Camp Shira, to make summer plans. Braving conditions that should have kept him at home, and motivated by a (now tentative) return flight that evening, Josh carefully drove his father-in-law's Ford Taurus down one-way Avenue N in Flatbush. Traffic was sparse — but suddenly,

Josh's rear-view mirror was filled with the menacing image of a van barreling down the street.

Because of the snow and the plowed remains, there wasn't enough room for the two of them, but Josh could tell from the van's rapid clip that it was hardly about to slow down. Had he attempted to brake he would have skidded on the ice and rammed into a row of parked cars.

Thus, Josh did what most drivers would have done in similar circumstances. He cleared to the right, held his breath and prayed for a modest collision.

His prayer was fulfilled.

He heard a crunch and felt the impact — not from the left where he had expected it, but from the *right*. The Taurus' right, side-view mirror, had connected with the mirror on the driver's side of a red Porsche. But this was no garden-variety, used Porsche. Not at all.

It was the recently released 911 Carrera 4S. Designed for the race track with

450 horsepower, 0-60 in 4.1 seconds, dynamic engine mounts, dual tailpipes and aerodynamics with even more downforce than most drag racers, the 911 is barely homologated for the road. MSRP a mere $93,200.00.

Taking the sticker price and dividing by inches, the damage that Josh had inflicted was easily a four-digit figure. The sirens that went off cacophonously in his head were joined by the car alarm that began to wail a mournful lament of the car's side-view mirror, now hanging precipitously by a single tendon.

Josh noticed a temporary paper license plate in the window featuring the date of issuance: February 11 — just the day before! The car was brand new and probably did not have more than ten miles driven on it. It was a beauty of a car with a major bloody nose.

With the alarm screeching, Josh assumed that the owner would be out any minute, but maybe because of the cold, or because sirens sound constantly in Gotham, no one emerged. Josh called Malka on his cell phone and asked her to come out, as he was only a few doors down.

Malka took one look at the glistening car and observed, "This doesn't belong to anyone on this block! If I were you," she suggested, "I wouldn't stick around."

"I can't do that," Josh protested. "It was an accident, but I hit him."

"I really don't think you should stay here," Malka insisted.

"I can't just walk away — I have to let him know I did it."

"Are you kidding?" Malka yelped. "This is New York! The guy'll kill you! Plus, if you stay out here any longer you'll freeze. So either way, you're finished!"

"You go back to your house," Josh instructed, "and I'll be in real soon."

JOSH PARKED HIS CAR and joined Malka inside. Before she could even serve him a hot drink he requested a piece of paper and wrote a note, which he placed on the

Porsche. Only afterward did he allow himself to get down to the business that had brought him to Brooklyn.

Josh still felt guilty even after leaving the note, and deliberately positioned himself in a chair facing the street. After nearly two hours, he saw what must have been the owner peering at his car and... crying. The man, in his early thirties, was barefoot and wearing nothing but shorts.

Josh pointed to the figure, but Malka claimed that she did not know who he was. Even had the man been wearing clothes, she assured Josh, she would not have recognized him.

Josh threw on his coat and headed for the door, despite Malka's desperate pleas to reconsider. Josh silently walked over to the man who was breathing steam, slapping his sides for warmth and heaving as he sobbed industrial-strength tears.

"Is this your car?" asked Josh. Not the most brilliant inquiry, but a good opening line nonetheless.

Nick Accardo replied, to no one in particular, "Brand new, brand NEW! I just got it; I just got it!"

Josh wondered if he were hearing an echo.

"Can you believe it? I don't even have it one day and look! If I get my hands on that—"

"I'm really sorry," Josh interjected at this critical juncture. "I'm so sorry, but I hit your car. It was an accident. I've been waiting here to find the owner for about an hour and a half."

Suddenly Nick stopped heaving and started blinking as though the falling snow were actually freshly-diced onions. "No way. You're messin' with me."

"Like I said, I'm really so—"

"No way, no way," Nick said, again displaying his propensity for repetition. "I really, really don't believe you, dude; you from New Yawk?"

Suddenly, a woman — also not dressed for the weather but clad more appropriately than Accardo's extreme — appeared across the street and Nick called out to her, "Carmela, this guy hit my car!"

Carmela unleashed a barrage of coarse language, sprinkling a few choice words like Parmesan on pasta, until Nick stopped her. "He hit me an hour and a half ago and he's been waiting here to tell me."

"You ain't from New Yawk, are ya," Carm affirmed, rolling her eyes in wonder.

Nick turned to Josh. "Nick Accardo, who're you?"

"Josh Stern. I'd like to give you the insurance details, but don't you think we should, er, do this inside?"

Either Nick didn't hear Josh's suggestion or it didn't register, but he had one thing to say and he repeated it several times. "I promise you, I will not take more than the repair cost. Not a penny!"

Josh supplied him with his father-in-law's insurance information and apologized once again for all the grief he had caused.

Three weeks later, Josh's father-in-law received the following letter in the mail:

"Dear Mr. Wasserman,

I wish to share my feelings with you about your son-in-law, Josh Stern, and my car. As you know, it was my car that Josh accidentally hit on Wednesday, February 12. I've lived in New York all my life, and I guess — as they say — we New Yorkers have an attitude problem. I am aware of this. And I do expect things to go a certain way.

But on that cold, wintry day, a day that I will never forget, Josh changed my philosophy. More importantly, he changed my attitude.

It was an emotional time for my sister and me for reasons Josh could not have known. My mother had died suddenly the night before and at a time when I was basically angry at the world, Josh taught me that there are still individuals with a sense of responsibility, fair play, fundamental integrity and kindness.

The aggravation I went through with the car repair was more than worth it for this lesson and for the privilege of meeting an unassuming, honest person like your son-in-law. I told many people at my mother's funeral about what Josh had done and everyone was very impressed with his honor and humanity.

My thanks to you and yours for restoring some faith to a man who had little of it to begin with. I know that in Heaven, my mother is smiling because of Josh's kindness and uprightness.

My mother always felt that I was too critical and mistrusting (she was neither born nor raised in NY). Therefore, even though the events of that Wednesday delayed me, I trust that she will forgive me for being late to her wake.

Respectfully,
Nicholas Accardo

Heard from: Yosef Weiss

Beloved

Lost and Found

*L*IKE SO MANY other parents preparing to visit their children in the Holy Land, the Zalatanskys were furiously shopping, bent on fulfilling their offspring's wish list for American-brand products that cannot be obtained (or are just too expensive) in the heart of the Middle East.

The modest requests of their son and daughter-in-law were viewed merely as points of departure. Their actual fulfillment would expand depending on what was available at several local malls. The net result of these forays to a battery of stores was enough luggage to fill the hull of an ocean liner. Yet the Zalatanskys intended to take it all with them on their El Al flight.

Far greater than the challenge of the airline's weight limitation was the Law of Conservation of Matter that all but forbade the inclusion of so much physical stuff in so little space. But the Zalatanskys were not going to allow a technicality like a law of nature stand in their way. Hence they spent several agonizing contortion sessions stretching, pulling and sitting to get their suitcases closed. The result was a matching set of giant vinyl-clad Chiclets, pillow-shaped things on skateboard wheels that they pulled behind them, pet-like, on leashes.

There was the big suitcase, the overweight suitcase, the mega-overweight suitcase and the small one, that really wasn't small, but it would be the first one on the scale to dupe the hostess at check-in to believing that all of the luggage was moderate and within the weight limit. Then there were the carry-ons that were just as heavy as their stalwart non-onboard companions but required micro-precision packing to insert contents never designed for such close quarters, again defying all natural laws. Suits and coats and dresses were rolled and stuffed into swollen pouches crisscrossed by zippers, bulbous and warty all over with shoe pockets looking like bloated life vests. And of course there was the *shaitel* (wig) box of brown faux-alligator vinyl that is going to play a seminal role in this story.

Check-in was blessedly uneventful, and none of the charm routines that the Zalatanskys had rehearsed in their heads had to be activated. The flight, too, as far as international travel goes, was pleasant. Best of all, the entire Jerusalem Zalatansky gang was there to greet them at the airport, and embracing grandchildren who had grown up so much since the last visit was an indescribable pleasure.

With their luggage hastily loaded into a taxi, the reunited Zalatanskys headed up to the Holy City. In minutes the Senior Zalatanskys had left their trip behind them, and the conversation was non-stop, catching up on lives that were separated by nearly 7,000 miles.

DANNY HAD arranged an apartment for his parents adjacent to his, in the Maalot Dafna section of Jerusalem. Thus, the taxi only had to make one stop to let off both families. The plan was that the seniors would get settled and then join the juniors for a late supper in half an hour. But the settling proved to be unsettling as the *shaitel* box, the one with the brown vinyl imitation alligator design, wasn't there.

"Marty, where's my *shaitel* box?" Rivka inquired.

"It's probably with the other luggage in the entranceway," her husband responded absently.

"No, it's not there either; I'm sure of that."

"Then I'll go outside. May be we forgot to bring it in."

Marty went out to the spot where the taxi had dropped them off, but there was nothing there but plastic bags and candy wrappers that the wind blew about his ankles. Just to be sure, he dropped by Danny's to see if by accident the *shaitel* box had ended up there. Alas, it had not.

Marty returned home and gave Rivka his update, propelling her into an anxiety attack. "So where could you have put it?" she demanded.

"Rivka, honestly, *shaitel*s are not my department. I'm sure that it was not in the taxi, for I personally unloaded all of the bags from the car. And I can't imagine that we left it on the luggage trolley in the airport."

"So then where could it be? Tomorrow is already Shabbos!"

Rivka Zalatansky, the co-star of this story, is your average even-keeled woman who is calm and collected — except when her expensive dress *shaitel* goes missing on a Thursday night in a foreign country. Marty Zalatansky is not your average even-keeled man, he is colossally even-keeled and virtually nothing can rock his even keel, certainly not a missing *shaitel*. He has the presence of a male flight attendant, overly pleasant and calm. At work they call him the "fireman," for he is always extinguishing potentially explosive or combustible situations.

After scratching their heads — Rivka, anxiously, and Marty, patiently — they concluded that they must have left the *shaitel* in the overhead compartment of the plane. There should still be time, even on a short winter Friday, to retrieve it.

Little did the Zalatanskys know that Friday in Israel is akin to Sunday in America and most offices, including Ben Gurion Airport's Lost and Found, are closed. Rivka wore her weekday *shaitel* that Shabbos.

FIRST THING Sunday morning, Marty was on the phone with Lost and Found. The clerk flatly denied having anything even remotely akin to a brown simulated-leather wig box, but offered to look around again. Marty was issued a claim number corresponding to their flight and was advised to call again the next day. Number in hand, the Zalatanskys called Lost and Found no less than seven times between Monday morning and Wednesday evening. Each time a different clerk denied the existence of the box, but vowed that the search would continue.

Despair began to hover in the air like the Angel of Doom, as a week had already elapsed and not a single clue to the whereabouts of the wig box had turned up. Meanwhile, Shabbos was once again approaching, and Rivka had only her weekday *shaitel*. Exacerbating matters was the fact that Rivka was in the beginning of her year of mourning for her mother and was not allowed to opt for the most efficient, albeit expensive, solution: buying a new *shaitel*. For the next ten months, no new expensive items would be gracing Rivka's wardrobe.

For the uninformed reader, such a wig can cost in excess of $1800 — not counting cutting, fitting, perming and treating. The loss was grand, the anguish great and the frustration resulting from the daily discussions with the callous Lost and Found clerks, excruciating.

Day after day, conversations with Lost and Found went like this:

"Allo."

"I'm calling regarding a lost object that was left in an overhead bin above seat 42C on El Al flight 002 from New York on November 29. The file number is J44C1L..."

"Allo."

"I said that I was inquiring about file number—"

"No speak *Angleet*. You vait."

(Two minutes later) "Allo."

"Hello Ma'am, as I was telling the gentleman before you, I would like you to check on claim J44C1L—"

"I don't work in Lost and Found."

"Then why was I transferred to you?"

"Do I sound like a philosopher? Do I speak like a psychologist?" Click.

"Did I just speak to you about—"

"No speak to me, no speak *Angleet*; I give you Evleen."

"Hello, this is Evelyn."

"Finally, someone who speaks English," Marty sighed.

"Well, I've been living in Israel for thirty-one years, but still haven't forgotten my mother tongue," the middle-aged voice continued. "How can I help you? Oh, I know. You're the guy who called about the baby stroller, right?"

"No, that wasn't me."

But as Evelyn had recently become a grandmother and was shopping for strollers, she was very much up on the subject. So much so that she thought that everyone else was talking about strollers, too. "So let me ask you some questions. We have several strollers here and these models cost a pretty penny. Beats me how people could walk out of the airport without their stroller; but, hey, I'm only working Lost and Found, not Parenting 101 —"

"Evelyn, please listen to me. I'm not missing—"

"Trust me, there is no one in this entire department that *listens* better than me. That's why I am going through all this trouble. First thing I want you to do is describe the fabric."

"You mean of the wig box?"

"Call it whatever you like. You'd be surprised what people call these things. Why the Brits call them pr—"

Marty got so excited that he had a native English-speaker on the line, he focused on whatever he thought could lead to their salvation, and ignored nuances and intimations that should have indicated otherwise.

"It is brown simulated-alligator skin," Marty chanted.

"I see that description is not your strong suit. The closest to what you describe I would call Cappuccino Brown."

"So you mean you found it?!"

"Found three; it could be there's more.

There are piles and piles of junk here."

"All of them brown?"

"No, aside from the Cappuccino, there is also a Sunrise Navy and a Bubblegum Pink."

"You mean to say that there is a wig box that is pink?"

"I mean you would flip your wig if you were to see this item: water bottle holder, snack tray, reclining seat, sun canopy—"

"I'm sorry, there must be a mistake."

"Mistake is the understatement of the season! How could someone forget a thing like this in the airport? Height adjustable handles, padded harness, front swivel wheel..."

"Lady, please! I appreciate your enthusiasm, but I'm not looking to buy a stroller. I just want our wig—"

"You wear a wig?! Well... it doesn't matter, and I'm not prying — hey, to each their own." There was a momentary pause and then Evelyn went back to the thread she'd just lost, describing the assets of the strollers piled around her: "Ergonomically designed, folds easily, light-weight..."

Even ultra-even-keeled Marty had to pull the plug on this one.

THE ZALATANSKYS eventually concluded that their only hope was to actually go down to the airport and look for the wig box. However, in no way did their plan conform with airport regulations or the overall reality of Israeli bureaucracy that deems any approach akin to "the customer is always right" as fundamentally foreign.

To somehow vindicate this excursion, whose outcome seemed bleakly predictable, they decided to combine it with a visit to the cemetery in Bnei Brak where Rivka's grandmother was buried. Following this they would call upon Marty's aunt (whom in fact they called to inform of their visit) who lived near the cemetery.

Items two and three of the itinerary were a cakewalk. Item one, they learned — to put it very kindly — was as likely as bouncing a bowling ball. Any plans they had of simply entering the Lost and Found and inspecting the merchandise were summarily dismissed by airport protocol — Israeli airport protocol, that is, for they had already been exposed to the Lost and Found in Newark Airport in the past and the difference was profound.

Newark Airport's Lost and Found, even though it was located in the Police Administration Building, underneath the control tower no less, was as accessible as a supermarket. The clerk had been playing a game on his cell phone when they arrived, so oral communication was out of the question. All he could do was point with his head for them to enter and have a look around.

In Ben Gurion Airport, very safely removed from the control tower, was *Fort* Lost and Found. There were probably few Israeli generals on active duty that had the security clearance to gain entry. So how can an ordinary citizen get inside to see if his backpack or wig box was enshrined there?

The short answer is, he can't. The Israelis

have developed a clever system to simultaneously guarantee security and ensure that no specimen of mankind would ever attempt to enter the inner sanctum. Just to be sure, a number of lengthy regulations and intimidations are posted to protect the lost items from ever being reconnected with their rightful owners.

First in the line of obstruction is the impregnable glass booth, only rarely staffed by a worker whose job it is to service people requiring Lost and Found. His or her absence contributes significantly to the air of despair intended to grip you. Communication with the non-existent guard— or any other truly incorporeal Lost and Found workers that are truly out of sight — is achieved by calling from a phone that is conveniently located on the wall nearby. But as there is no dial tone, you never know if there is actually a person on the other end. A sign near the phone offers instructions in Hebrew that are as comprehensible, even for one versant in the language, as an explanation of the Bosch fuel-injection system.

Marty gazed glumly at the sheer neglect

of the Lost and Found glass booth. Even the newspaper folded on the counter was yellowed.

He picked up the telephone receiver and waited. He waited and waited until a clerk competing for the Lost and Found sound-alike contest finally barked, "Allo!"

"Could you please connect me with the Lost and Found?" Click-click, ring-ring, buzz, click-click, followed by a long buzz that morphed into a ring with European urgency. The urgency was apparently lost on the other end but eventually a human, from the actual Lost and Found department, answered. Even-keeled Marty patiently inquired, "Could you please look up case number J44C1L? I am here in the airport, and I would like to personally search for my very valuable item."

Something about Marty's request — perhaps it was his accent, or the outrageous innocence of his query — made it sound like the greatest joke the clerk had ever heard, and he broke into raucous laughter. Quickly controlling himself, he instructed, "Just take a seat and call back in a few minutes to see if there is any need to visit the Lost and Found."

With some time on his hands, Marty joined Rivka in the arrivals section of the airport. The hall had become a total zoo, as the Israeli soccer team was due to arrive back home after a key victory. The space was packed with fans, and their behavior was a tad on the rowdy side, enhanced by beverage intake. Fifteen minutes later, just as word leaked out — faster than radiation from a government reactor — that the team was about to appear, Marty knew that it was time to resume his mission. Regrettably, he would have to miss the excitement, but he was sure Rivka would apprise him regarding his loss.

Marty dutifully called back and this time he was directed to an intercom, yet another obstacle in the Maginot Line of Obstruction to the Lost and Found. Yelling into a wall in a public place does wonders for your resolve. A faceless voice crackled back from the wall that the item was not there, and furthermore, the faceless voice asserted, he had even spoken to his supervisor about it. "Perhaps," Marty offered, "the item has not been coded correctly? It would be so productive if I could just come in and look for myself, since I would recognize the box right away."

This is where the Wall of Obstruction garnered additional fortification; external penetration was verboten. The faceless voice said as much.

There was no reason, the faceless voice asserted, to violate protocol and allow Marty in when there wasn't even a doubt regarding the lost item's presence. It was most regrettable that the item was lost, but that did not, perforce, mean that it was located in the Lost and Found.

MARTY didn't know gimmicks, he didn't know leveraging, he didn't know how to threaten to higher ups — he only knew how to speak the truth. And that is exactly what he tried to do, to a most unsympathetic audience. He also tried to impress upon the faceless voice the extenuating circumstances caused by Rivka's period of mourning — and all of this, shouting into a perforated piece of plastic screwed to the wall in a crowded public place where hundreds of tipsy soccer fans were cheering and erupting into jigs of joy.

For all of his sincerity, Marty's strategy was ineffective. A lost wig-box that wasn't turned in to them — even if it should have been — as well as Mrs. Zalatansky's period of mourning were simply not their problem. Goodbye.

As noted earlier, Marty Zalatansky is a mild-mannered individual and his patience was met with repugnance; his persistence with intolerance. The Lost and Found maintained that the *shaitel* was not there, and requesting to search for it himself was being considered as favorably as was the Black Plague in Sweden.

Marty broke the news to his wife that, aside from being present for the national soccer team homecoming, they had nothing to show for their trip to the airport. Just then the team's famed goalie emerged to tumultuous applause, and an autograph clot formed as a forest of pens sprang forth. Tens of arms were outstretched and mouths, open like baby birds awaiting supper, cawed "Azulai! Azu-lai!"

The roar of the fans seemed to deride the Zalatankys' frustrating excursion with smug satisfaction. The two of them sat there in stunned silence as they pondered their next step. Then Rivka, as if oblivious to all that had transpired, requested that her husband try one last time.

There wasn't much that Marty would have preferred to do less. But seeing how despondent his wife was, he caved in. For a final time Marty approached the obstacle field and, lo and behold, there was a clerk sitting in the perpetually unmanned booth. The lady was working on her nails and obviously did not appreciate being interrupted. Before Marty even had a chance to turn on the charm, the clerk emitted enough disdain-firepower to wipe out a busload of Peace Corps volunteers. And that's before he opened his mouth! Once he said "hello" it was all downhill.

The lady was aware that he had attempted to be allowed into the Lost and Found before, and told him not to approach the intercom. *She* was going to handle this, and that did not augur well.

Marty was sure that the powers-that-be must have realized that he would try to get in again, and they had sent up their strongest candidate for Miss Congeniality to dissuade him. He saw her punch a button, followed by discussion. Although he could neither hear nor decipher what was being said, her menacing facial expressions did not require interpretation.

She hung up the phone and snarled. Because Lost and Found employees know that no one comes to them who is not upset, they believe, and work hard to show, that it is a two-way street. Nothing riles them up more than someone who refuses to get riled up. Before Marty got to say much of anything, she informed him matter-of-factly that it was impossible for him to be admitted into Fort Lost and Found.

But Marty was fueled by the fact that he had nothing to lose, and he dug in his heels. He had traveled all the way to the airport in search of a valuable item; why couldn't they give him the satisfaction of knowing that it truly wasn't there?

This clerk would have none of it and

annoyance spewed out of her like the spray from a hydrant wrenched open in the summertime. The fact that he wouldn't back down proved to be, most remarkably, an effective strategy. Suddenly, the worker glanced up from her nails and actually looked Marty in the face. She then put on the kind of smile that funeral directors would pay good money to master.

"You may go to the gate," she intoned, "and someone from the Lost and Found will pick you up," and with that she was back to filing her fingernails.

Marty's jaw went slack. Suddenly he felt like one of the ubiquitous soccer fans. He was really excited, but there was a tinge of reality that sobered his relief. True, the trip to the airport had now been vindicated and he might be able to alleviate some of Rivka's dejection, but the odds of finding the *shaitel* box in the Lost and Found were still slim.

After waiting at the gate for a full ten minutes, a nice young lady arrived and explained the security hurdles that would have to be overcome in order to gain entry to the Lost and Found. The office was located inside the terminal proper, adjacent to the luggage carousels. This would involve the submission of his passport, signing a written affidavit attesting to the fact that he had a valid reason for entering the inner terminal, and undergoing a security interview.

The entire time, his escort, who was a trainee and hence not yet hardened by the rigors of work, stood by his side and walked him through the process literally and figuratively. Finally they arrived at Fort Lost and Found.

OUTSIDE the actual office were mounds of luggage that had obviously not yet been processed. Inside there were five workers slumped over their computers watching what appeared to be web-related features not readily connected with the Lost and Found. The trainee brought Marty over to one of the workers in order to fill out a form detailing his missing object. Marty subsequently learned that this was to keep him honest, lest he find something in the storage room and feign that it was what he had been looking for.

The completed form was handed to a Russian lady who matched the contents with the information on file for claim number J44C1L. As soon as everything was in sync, Marty was granted permission to enter the critical inner-sanctum of the fort.

Marty was imagining a hall of fun-house mirrors that would make *shaitel* boxes appear like baby strollers. But before he even actually entered the cavernous room to check his hypothesis... there, right before his eyes, smack dab in the middle of the entranceway was the distinctive *shaitel* box.

"This is it!" Marty practically screamed to the kind trainee who was escorting him, as he broke into a crazy dance. Even-keeled Marty Zalatansky had lost his even and had lost his keel, and he hugged everyone of male persuasion in the vicinity.

Alas, either because of protocol or because of his histrionics, the Lost and Found staff still required additional proof that the box, the very one that he had perfectly described orally and in writing for a full week, was indeed his.

Obviously there were numerous charlatans that sought a wig combed and set for a middle-plus-aged grandmother, and one could never be too careful — not to mention that bulky, brown, simulated-alligator-leather boxes strong enough to hold no more than a wig and Styrofoam head were in high demand. Hey, without proof-positive, someone looking for a bubblegum-pink baby stroller may walk out with a brown wig-box. You just could never be too careful.

But before the Lost and Found clerk could launch an investigation, the matter was resolved. Inside the box there was a small pink slip from the *shaitel-macher* upon which she had written the name "Zalatansky." True, there could be many Zalatanskys out there claiming a brown simulated-leather *shaitel* box, but the L&F detectives generously did not press the case.

Marty, even-keeled all over again, tried to soberly assess the situation. For an entire week he was consistently told that the most prominently positioned item in the storeroom wasn't there at all. Marty imagined that at that moment a healthy portion of humble pie should be served at the Lost and Found, yet the workers seemed remarkably unfazed by their ineptitude. The Russian clerk offered weakly, "I did not know that you were on *that* flight; I thought you were on today's flight."

But why would she, why would anyone, offer such an inane excuse? Every time he called, he submitted the file number along with the flight and its date. Could it be that workers had become so exposed to the unlikelihood of finding a lost object that they only went through the motions of restoration? Marty could see that the trainee was also troubled and embarrassed by the apathy and inefficiency that had surrounded his case.

A reckoning with the L&F staff was indicated, not to rub their noses in their ineptitude or to engage in one-upmanship, which would have been so out of character for Marty, but to effect an improvement in their modus operandi. The image of all of the items lying about the room, and the anguish this represented to so many individuals, would undoubtedly haunt him; he was already vexed by the futility of his own numerous phone calls. Rousing himself from his thoughts, he realized that he could ill-afford these ruminations, as long as Rivka was still agonizing over her loss.

Marty was sure that once he showed her the treasure in his hand, the excited throngs in the hall would think that she, too, was a soccer fan. He was mistaken, though. Once Rivka spotted her husband, the soccer fans were clearly the *least* excited individuals in the airport. She let out a whoop and then raised her hands as if she were a prize-fighter who had just won a knockout after nine long rounds.

Before departing, Marty felt duty-bound to at least show the clerk in the glass booth that his persistence had been vindicated. Alas, she was no longer there, obviously having been called back to Fort Lost and Found for vital work, leaving the booth manned by fundamentally the same indifference.

MARTY AND RIVKA, with victory in their corner, departed the terminal, Bnei Brak-bound, with bells on their toes and wings on their backs. After a brief stop for

Minchah and a falafel, they grabbed a taxi to the cemetery, aware of how inappropriately they felt for such a somber place.

The sky over Bnei Brak was the color of wet newspaper, and it was safe to assume that in the near future, everything underneath it would be wet as well. Thus, with fervor and sincerity, and not a whole lot of time, Marty and Rivka offered up their devotions. As an extra measure of gratitude was indicated, they concluded their *Tehillim* at the gravesite of Rav Shach.

Just as the Zalatanskys were wondering how to escape the impending rain, a car roared into the cemetery and parked on the path next to Rav Shach's tombstone. Leaving the engine running, the young driver darted out to recite a quick chapter of *Tehillim* at the grave. As he was diving back into the driver's seat, Marty glanced up at the clouds and then at the gate, a full football field away. There was no language barrier in the question behind his raised eyebrow. The driver waved them in and before the Zalatanskys had even closed the back door, the car sped off, coming to a screeching halt at the main gate. Marty and Rivka got out to wash their hands.

Obviously the driver was late for a very important date, for by the time Rivka turned around, the driver had long departed. "Where's the car?!" she gasped.

"What do you need the car for?" Marty inquired. A wave of gray passed over him when he saw the darkness in Rivka's eyes as she solemnly pronounced that she had left the *shaitel* box in the car.

"But why did you leave it in the car?" Marty wanted to know.

"I didn't know that he was stopping to let us out; I was sure that after we washed our hands we would get back in." A terrible gulf of misunderstanding had just ruined what had promised to be the sunniest shower. Marty darted out to the street in the hope that he might catch the driver at a red light, but the car was not to be seen.

Somberly, Marty returned to the graveyard and Rivka feared that her husband would have a heart attack right then and there from the aggravation that she had caused. After all that he had done to recover her *shaitel*, it was now headed into the unknown at breakneck speed. But Rivka, of all people, should have been aware that her even-keeled husband, the proverbial "fireman," would not lose it over this.

Still, he was plagued by the conundrum, "What does God want from us?" They were getting a clear message, but they were not tuned into the proper frequency to decipher its meaning.

Although the rain appeared nanoseconds away, the two of them stood dumbstruck, at a total loss as to what their next step should be.

Their situation had, ironically, deteriorated even from the frustration of the day before. At least at the Lost and Found there was a specific address and a probable likelihood as to where the *shaitel* was. But they hadn't clue as to the young driver's identity.

Marty's assessment was that nothing about the driver's deportment indicated that he would be inspecting his car and heading back to return that which wasn't his. Nevertheless, they left their phone number with the caretaker at the cemetery, with the sinking feeling that this was even less productive than describing a *shaitel* box to someone gushing about baby strollers.

By this point, they were in no mood to visit their aunt. If only they hadn't notified her ahead of time, they would have been able to skip a stop for which they had no patience. The two of them just brooded and even the pouring rain could not prod them to take cover.

FINALLY, slowly and reluctantly, they made their way to a house full of relatives who would expect them to smile and giggle about family-related trivia. The entire way there, they attempted to properly comprehend the obscure message that God was sending them. What was He trying to tell them?

The problem with celestial phone calls is that even when you hear the ring, you're never quite sure how to pick up the receiver. Perhaps, the thought recurred all-too-frequently, it was a sign that it was inappropriate for Rivka to wear a wig and that she should cover her hair with a *tichel*.

The assembly at the aunt's house was better and worse than they had anticipated. Worse, insofar as there were more relatives squeezed into the apartment than they had imagined and the atmosphere was too convivial for their moods. Better, in so far as it was cathartic to relate their dismal story and unburden it a little from their chests. The tale definitely had its lighter moments, but Rivka's morose state put a clamp on the laughter.

Still, everyone tried to top it with their own tales of Murphy's Law. Marty actually said in his rendition that they were simultaneously *shlemiels* and a *shlemazels*, and it looked like this was the way they would forever be remembered in the annals of family history.

Someone suggested that they make a large sign with their contact information and hang it up at the entrance to the cemetery. This was followed by many other suggestions. All the assembled conducted an impromptu brainstorming session to decide what steps could be implemented to locate the elusive *shaitel*. One offered to print flyers that could be handed out and posted in public places so that whoever discovered the *shaitel* box would know where to call.

Others proposed placing an announcement in the religious newspapers. That suggestion was received with favor, until someone erroneously volunteered the information that they had already missed the deadline for that week and would need to wait until Sunday. Nevertheless, it was a good suggestion. Marty and Rivka were bolstered by their relatives' show of support, and they hoped that all was not lost — no pun intended.

THE ZALATANSKY JUNIORS in Jerusalem were taking it as hard as their parents. They, too, tried to come up with a plan of action. Little did they know that at the exact same time, a woman of action in Bnei Brak was about to thicken the plot. Chanita Bellin is her name and perseverance is her game.

That fateful Thursday night, Chanita went out to her car and noticed a *shaitel* box that she did not recognize. Assuming that it must belong to one of her daughters, she gave each of them a call and was perplexed to hear that no one was missing a *shaitel*.

This got Chanita scratching her own *shaitel*. How could a mysterious *shaitel* just appear in her car? She remembered that she had lent the car that afternoon to a boy who was a frequent guest of theirs. Why he, of all people, would leave a *shaitel* in the back seat was baffling, but it was a start.

It also seemed like a finish, since the boy claimed that he had not left anything in the car. But Chanita would not dismiss the matter. She subjected him to a thorough interrogation as to what he did while he had the car. But the investigation went nowhere for he claimed that he had a lot to do and little time to do it in, and at no point did he give anyone a ride.

Sherlock Chanita was not going to let this pass. What the boy had said made sense and was consistent, but there was a *shaitel* box in her car that refuted his story! So she started all over again: what did he do and where did he go for every minute that he'd had the car?

The interrogation wore on, until he remembered giving a mini-ride to a middle-aged couple in the cemetery. But this, he asserted with full conviction, could not explain the mystery, for they did not have anything with them. He neglected to add that his tremendous rush had not allowed for any attention to details.

Chanita dismissed the witness and widened her probe. She discovered the same identity-verifying slip of pink paper that said "Zalatansky." This wasn't much to go on, but she was relieved that it didn't say "Cohen" or "Katz."

Mrs. Bellin drew a few conclusions that put time at a premium for returning the *shaitel* to its undoubtedly desperate owner. This was not your garden-variety *shaitel*. The quality and the way that it was coiffed led her to conclude that it was for a special occasion. The fact that the name was written in English informed her that the owner must be a tourist visiting Israel for a *simcha*, and there was scant little time to get the *shaitel* back to its headlord before Shabbos.

With characteristic speed, Chanita ripped open the phonebook and called up each of the four Zalatanskys that were listed, but none of them had a relative visiting from abroad. She then called each of the area hotels, but none of them had a guest by the name of Zalatansky. As a last resort, she called up the local religious newspapers and placed a posting about the lost wig. At that point, she could think of nothing else that she could do. She was confident that the frenetic loser would be scanning the listings in the Friday editions of the papers.

But when the clock struck 11:00 Friday morning and her phone had still not rung, Chanita Bellin began to panic. It never occurred to her that she had really done all that she could do. She seemed to be equally unperturbed by the fact that it was a short Friday and the eve of Shabbos Chanukah, when many guests would be arriving at her home and dining at her table. She knew but one thing: time was running out for poor Mrs. Zalatansky, whoever she was. Poor Mrs. Zalatansky and her husband, in the meantime, were still under the misconception that the Friday paper went to press before the *shaitel* went missing and therefore did not do the obvious.

But time, historically, always marches forward and when it neared noon, Chanita, in a fit of anxiety, got hold of the Lost and Found numbers for each city. These are the numbers provided by a volunteer organization that attempts to fulfill the mitzvah of returning lost objects. Chanita flipped to Bnei Brak and punched in the number.

Her efforts were rewarded by being connected to the Lost and Found voice-mail options. In a voice that kept sinking to prayer level, it whispered, "If you lost a wallet, press 1; if you lost a book, press 2; if you lost a sweater, press 3..." Trying to find the *shaitel* category was like looking for a chicken's lips.

After listening to a lengthy listing of the various possibilities, she concluded that pressing "6" would be her best bet, since its category seemed to be closest to "lost wigs." But no matter how many times she pressed "6," the extension was always busy. She subsequently discovered that this was true for every other extension as well.

Shabbos was nearing and she was lost in the Lost and Found. Frantic, Chanita Bellin then started calling any number in the directory and actually reached a human voice for the Haifa Lost and Found, which was in fact located in Jerusalem. With volunteer organizations, you often get what you pay for.

ILANA WESTREICH in Jerusalem was as totally in the dark about lost items in Bnei Brak as she was, ironically, about lost items in Haifa. She got the job by *being* volunteered after a bizarre phone call. A *hashavas aveidah* operative, randomly scanning names in a phone book, called up the Westreichs and asked the lady who answered the phone if she would like to take part in the mitzvah of returning lost items.

Ilana never refuses a mitzvah opportunity, although she had no idea what she was agreeing to. "All you have to do," said the caller, "is simply (the word that always warns about impending disaster) be a matchmaker between losers and finders in your region." Being that all of the premier locations were already taken, Ilana was to be in charge of Haifa — a city she had never even visited.

But hey, you can't be a national organization if you only service Jerusalem, Bnei Brak, Kiryat Sefer and Beitar. From the day Ilana accepted this mitzvah, she had amassed a list spanning dozens of pages of items lost, and an equal number of pages listing items found, but never had she been able to match up one with the other.

Tenacious Mrs. Bellin was very excited to actually reach a human being and wasted no time in explaining why she was calling. "But you have reached the Haifa district; I don't work with Bnei Brak..." Ilana wanted to say, but she couldn't even slip in a syllable. Several times Ilana attempted to interrupt her insistent caller, but she was simply no match for Bellin. Chanita was determined to get the *shaitel* back to its rightful head before Shabbos, and she wasn't about to allow a mere technicality to stand in her way.

When Chanita Bellin finally came up for air, Ilana meekly offered to provide her with a non-automatic phone number in Bnei Brak. As Ilana sifted through her papers for the number, she heard Mrs. Bellin mutter to herself, "Poor Mrs. Zalatansky, who doesn't have…"

When Ilana heard "Zalatansky" her ears perked up. There was a new young couple that had just moved in next door whose name was Zalatansky; maybe they would know how to trace the lost wig.

Ilana dispatched one of her children to ask their neighbors if they were aware of any Zalatanskys who may have misplaced a wig, but the Westreich youngster's rapid-fire Hebrew was too much for Chavi Zalatansky, whose knowledge of *Ivrit* hadn't much improved over the years. Chavi was busy trying to cook up an impressive spread for her in-laws. She had no idea what her neighbor's daughter was babbling about, and she was just about to dismiss the girl when she caught the word *"shaitel."* That one word set off a clangorous chime of bells and whistles, causing Chavi to drop what she was doing and run across the hall to her neighbor's apartment.

Mrs. Bellin was still holding the line when Chavi got there. It took no more than a few seconds for everyone to realize that, at last, a *shidduch* had been made. The *hashavas aveidah* organization was a little less religious than Israel's Airport Authority about releasing lost items and the description of the wig, its box, and that it had been left in a car were adequate identification.

Mrs. Bellin realized how Providential it was that she had been unable to connect with the Bnei Brak Lost and Found, for they would have never been able to lead her to the rightful owner. The major hurdle was now over but a transfer still had to be executed.

DANNY Zalatansky stepped into the drama with Bellin-esque determination. His parents didn't yet know that the wig had been located, and to spare them further anguish, the younger Zalatansky thought that it would be best, based on the track record, not to say anything until the *shaitel* was actually in hand. One more up and down might be one vacillation too many for his parents; he also wanted to surprise them by retrieving the *shaitel* before Shabbos.

This was a very tall order. With just two hours until Shabbos, how were they going to get a *shaitel* from Bnei Brak to Jerusalem which, depending on congestion, is at least 50 minutes away? Someone theorized that since it was Shabbos Chanukah they might actually be able to find an acquaintance going from Bnei Brak to the Holy City. But like many theories, this was theoretical.

Everyone they consulted was quick to dismiss the problem as "no sweat" since there would be so many people traveling; but no one could suggest a *single* specific person who was actually making the trip.

The flurry of phone calls that were placed had a *déjà-vu* association to them, and time was lapsing rapidly. A breakthrough was urgently needed and fortunately the Ad Hoc Locate-the-*Shaitel* Committee had not yet disbanded.

Mrs. Westreich had a son learning in a Bnei Brak yeshivah and she put him on the case. She couldn't have selected a better man for the mission. Aryeh Westreich raced from yeshivah to yeshivah canvassing for Jerusalemites who had not yet left for home. One lead led him to another lead which led him — at last — to a boy who was just about to depart for the Ramot section of Jerusalem. The *shaliach mitzvah* was cellphone-less so he provided Aryeh with his home number instead. The *Shaitel* Committee in Jerusalem calculated his travel time and pegged his ETA at about 20 minutes before candle lighting. If Danny could be waiting at the Ramot address things should *just* work out.

THE COURIER, however, in his hasty departure on the last Jerusalem-bound shuttle of the week, felt no compulsion to inform his family that he was not coming home empty-handed. Thus the boy's mother was surprised at first, and subsequently annoyed, by the repeated phone calls to know if a lady's wig had arrived. So annoyed, that she refused to reveal her residence to the Committee.

Meanwhile, a very subdued Rivka and Marty were planning to *daven* at the *Kotel* Friday night. But just as they were preparing to leave they got a phone call from Danny requesting that they come over right away to watch the kids light their menorahs. He was really very insistent.

Marty and Rivka walked to their children's apartment, passing families gathered around entranceways and crowded next to windows, preparing to kindle the Chanukah lights. The youngest Zalatanskys did a picture-perfect performance, followed by warm embraces and resounding Chanukah wishes. Marty could now leave for shul, but Danny announced, "Just one minute more, we have a gift for you."

Marty and Rivka were surprised, even awkwardly so, for it is much more usual for parents to present a gift to their children than the other way around. Right now they didn't need a gift; they needed a lost *shaitel*.

So when Danny came back to the living room with an all-too-familiar box held in his outstretched hands, Marty and Rivka went, basically, insane. For the tech-age touch it was all captured on video. And, one more time, even-keeled Marty lost his keel and the Zalatanskys celebrated a most enlightening and illuminating Chanukah in Jerusalem.

Heard from: Moish and Yossi Zicherman

Life Saver

RABBI Shlomo Zalman Auerbach *zt"l*. It's not often that a name can be a sentence, but by the time you are finished reading this, hopefully you will understand the punctuation.

His sensitivity and love for his fellow man were evident throughout his life. As a student at *Etz Chayim*, when other boys would approach him for help in understanding some difficult point, he would always smile encouragingly and move over to make room on the bench where he sat, saying modestly, "Come, sit down. I'm sure you understand it yourself, perhaps even better than I do. So let's go over it again, together. To tell you the truth, I don't really understand it either. Let's see, Rashi explains... and the *Tosafos* ask... and... There, you see? You understood it all along and didn't need me after all."

Reb Shlomo Zalman educated the members of his family not to greatness and leadership (although there is no doubt he did that by example), but to genuine compassion. One who does not feel the pain of others, he maintained, is lacking not merely in *chessed*, but in his very humanity.

Reb Shlomo Zalman was perhaps most famous for his kindness to widows and orphans, but he sought out anyone in need. He would visit hospitals and old-age residences regularly, and it was not unusual to see him at a home for the mentally disabled. Strain or inconvenience were never factors when it came to visiting the disadvantaged or comforting mourners.

Reb Shlomo Zalman devoted his primary attention to embittered souls. The greater their affliction, the greater the priority he awarded them. A needy individual from a stable background would not merit as much attention as one with less wholesome credentials.

Reb Shlomo Zalman relished the role of father, and felt very natural filling it for whoever was lacking a father of his own. Even if there was a father, but he was absent or far away, Reb Shlomo Zalman would take a fatherly interest.

To the American students learning in a yeshiva near his home, he showed exceptional concern. He would ask them specific questions about their progress in their studies, about their adjustment to yeshivah life in Israel, and about their families abroad.

NO ONE will ever be able to quantify how much *chessed* Reb Shlomo Zalman did, for he worked "undercover," doing everything possible to avoid recognition. His foremost concern was that the recipient's privacy and dignity be maintained. Found among his records was a loan to a drug addict in the amount of NIS 1,500, lent on condition that he continue rehabilitation.

Reb Shlomo Zalman believed that it wasn't enough to compensate favors and services with money; it was essential to also treat the provider of such services with extreme courtesy and show a genuine interest in their work, and in them as individuals. A trenchant example of this was the way that he dealt with taxi drivers, whom he would always engage in conversation. Incapable of meaningless small talk, Reb Shlomo Zalman would raise a general topic and somehow manage to make the conversation elevating to the listener. Once, in a smoke-filled taxi, the topic of conversation was how to break the habit of smoking.

Taxi drivers loved Rabbi Auerbach and would vie for the honor of transporting him. One driver related, "I picked up Reb Shlomo Zalman over at Kol Torah. As usual, he climbed into the front seat and greeted me, calling me his *manhig*. I tried to explain to him that in Hebrew the word for 'driver' is *nahag* and that although the two words have the same root, *manhig* means 'leader.' I figured he was more accustomed to speaking Yiddish, so he wasn't aware of the subtleties of Hebrew grammar. But no — Reb Shlomo Zalman insisted that I was his *manhig* because I would 'lead' him to his destination. It was such a small thing, and yet it made me feel great. This important Rabbi considered me his *manhig*!...."

THERE I GO AGAIN, reminiscing (and engaging in self-plagiarism) about the spiritual giant whom I was privileged to know and learn from. There is one more story that I wish to share about my rebbe and since I (the author of the book you are holding) am a minor protagonist in the story, I shall indulge in the luxury of a first-hand rendition.

The 20th of Adar is the *yahrzeit* of Rabbi Auerbach, and on this date I was scheduled to speak in Silver Spring, Maryland. Since it was precisely two years since the Gaon's passing, I used the opportunity to recall before the august audience tales of the man who was clearly the people's choice: the one who merited the largest funeral in the history of the Jewish People.

Unbeknownst to me, there was a woman in the audience who had made extraordinary efforts to attend. She lived far away, was intrigued and ended up walking in excess of two miles to hear the lecture. In other words, if you wanted to fancy up the story, you could add that she wasn't supposed to be there, did not intend to go to that synagogue, "just happened" to overwalk from where she originally had in mind, etc. But hey, far be it from me to engage in that kind of storytelling...

The life of Reb Shlomo Zalman was so varied, rich and personable, that everyone can relate to the ways of this righteous man. But one of the stories that I conveyed during my talk hit— let's call her Tova Katz — like a ton of avalanching, iron-packed, concrete-reinforced bricks.

The story, which has been oft-quoted and infrequently attributed,* goes like this: Karen, an assimilated college student vacationing in Israel, had inadvertently stumbled across her religion and started attending a few classes to find out more about Judaism. Attending classes, of course, cannot be confused with adopting a religious

---

* *And From Jerusalem HIS Word*; stories and insights of Rabbi Shlomo Zalman Auerbach *zt"l*, Hanoch Teller, NYC Publishing Company, 1995.

lifestyle, and Karen was still in the very initial stages of discovering what Torah and *mitzvos* were all about.

One day, Karen ever-so-casually mentioned to a friend of hers that she was pregnant and was going to have an abortion. This friend brought the matter to the attention of Rabbi Stein in Jerusalem, whom Karen had become acquainted with over the previous few days.

Rabbi Stein was naturally upset when he heard this, but what could he say to dissuade a "liberated" young woman raised on a cultural doctrine of "Do your own thing," a woman who had yet to learn what a mitzvah *was*, let alone the obligation to observe it.

In a last-ditch effort, Rabbi Stein devised the following scheme: He explained to Karen that having this procedure close to the end of the first trimester was by no means free of risk. It was therefore incumbent upon her to seek the blessing of a "holy man" before undergoing the operation, and Karen saw no reason to object.

Rabbi Stein brought the young woman to see Reb Shlomo Zalman, and it goes without saying that his intention was anything *but* to get the Gaon's blessing for this venture. When the two were ushered into the Rav's study, Rabbi Stein provided the Gaon with a brief synopsis of the situation and then remained to serve as interpreter.

Reb Shlomo Zalman asked Karen why she had come to see him. The young woman replied that she was there to seek his blessing. The Rav asked, "A blessing for what?" and Karen explained that she was about to have her pregnancy terminated and since this procedure involved some danger she sought the great Rabbi's blessing for success, safety, and good health.

Reb Shlomo Zalman, however, was not swift in dispensing his blessing. First some questions had to be answered. "Why is it that you want this procedure done?"

Karen explained that she was planning to embark on a long course of study toward the career which she had chosen, and having a baby would only get in her way.

"What sort of career do you intend to pursue?" the Rav asked.

"I want to be a doctor," the young woman replied.

"I see," the Gaon remarked. "And why do you want to be a doctor?"

Karen launched into the standard speech of a medical school applicant, explaining that there was nothing more noble or altruistic than the field of medicine.

"And why is it," Reb Shlomo Zalman inquired, "that you hold medicine in such high esteem?"

"Why," she exclaimed, taken aback at having to explain all of this to a man of supposed intelligence and stature, "through medicine I'll be able to save lives!" The irony of her response apparently escaped her.

The Gaon just sat in his chair contemplating her answer, as if it were a revolutionary concept and a challenging one for him to grasp. Karen began to get a little fidgety.

She could not understand what the difficulty was. Gears and cogs that should have been meshing in her head appeared to be jammed in some kind of cerebral gridlock that prevented them from making the simple connections from one synapse to another.

Finally, after what seemed an eternity of cogitation, he asked the young mother-to-be, "What is so important about saving lives?"

Karen was stumped. Not at the answer — why, everyone knew that there was no greater value — but at this purportedly brilliant Rabbi's inability to comprehend something so elementary. She glanced at her interpreter to verify that she had understood him. Then she glanced at him to verify that *he* understood *her*.

Once she discerned that Reb Shlomo Zalman was in fact waiting for an answer to the question of why saving lives was so important, she let him have it: "There simply is nothing more important in the whole world. In the universe!"

The Gaon reflected on this as well, giving his guest time to let it all sink in. But still the cogs and gears were not turning.

Finally Karen woke up and smelled the coffee. "Oh, no," she said with a start. "This," she declared, pointing at her abdomen, "this is only a fetus, not a life."

Reb Shlomo Zalman awarded her a quizzical look. He made it clear that he was not clear about the distinction between a fetus and a life. "But you do agree," he asked most accommodatingly, "that a fetus will become a baby?"

Karen couldn't deny that, but she still maintained that currently it was not yet a life.

To this the Gaon asked, "What if I were to tell you that your baby is destined to become a great person?"

It did not take Karen long to respond. "There is no way of knowing if the baby will or won't become a great person."

"True," Reb Shlomo Zalman agreed,

appreciating her reply, "but you have only answered half the question. Why is it that there is no way of knowing how the baby will develop?"

"Because there are so many factors involved. Genetics, geography, nutrition, environmental influences, and so forth. It's basically a question of 'nature versus nurture'."

"But you certainly realize the kind of input that you as a mother and an intelligent person could have." Karen readily conceded this point.

"I am sure," the Rav asserted, "that the child will be bright, for you seem to be a clever individual. So the 'nature' is there; the factor that is in doubt is the surroundings, the role that the environment will play upon this child's upbringing.

"I therefore believe," Reb Shlomo Zalman continued with certitude, "that there are but two courses for you to follow with this child: Either you raise it, and nurture the baby with the love that it deserves and that you could certainly provide; or you give it to me. My name is Shlomo Zalman Auerbach, and you can ask around — I am pretty well known. I would be glad to see to it that your baby would not be denied the nurturing it deserves. But these are clearly the only two choices you have."

Karen repeated after him, as if reciting a mantra, "The only two choices, the only two choices..." Her brow furrowed, she seemed to fold inward into stony silence. At last she asked, "Do I have to make that decision now?"

Rabbi Stein could hardly believe the *question*. In a matter of two minutes Reb Shlomo Zalman, one unschooled in the methodology of *kiruv rechokim* and never briefed on how to zero in on the wavelength of a college kid devoid of a religious background, had accomplished the ultimate in auto-suggestion, as it is known. He had allowed her — a young woman who had merely come to seek a blessing before a "minor" clinical procedure — to figure out for herself that she really had only *one* choice: to have the baby. The Gaon had deftly maneuvered the conversation so that she had reached his conclusion on her own. Whether to keep her child or give him to a perfect stranger was, at this point, a question not even worthy of a question mark.

I MOVED ON in my memorial tribute to other questions that had been posed to Rabbi Auerbach, but I had left Tova Katz behind and nearly paralyzed by the howling winds of guilt rising out of deep uncharted canyons within her. Now she knew why she had walked so far to attend the talk: Reb Shlomo Zalman was talking to her!

Tova is an ultrasound technician working for a private medical group. Basically, what she does for a living, although most indirectly, is facilitate a stage in the process that results in abortions. Right then and there, she pledged to herself that the next time a Jewish woman came to her for an ultrasound, she would attempt to dissuade her from undergoing an abortion.

TWO DAYS LATER, a Russian lady entered the clinic for an ultrasound. Tova could not discern her religion from her name, but she did have Jewish features. This was Tova's moment of truth: her resolve in the synagogue had been strong, but now it was faltering precipitously. What she was about to do violated Maryland State Law and she felt a hard fist of fear grow in her stomach.

Tova took a deep breath and then, instead of greeting the woman in front of her with pleasantries and uttering the standard procedural instructions, she asked in a barely audible tone, "Are you Jewish?"

The woman nodded affirmatively, apparently not the least upset by the inquiry. Tova was unsure of her next move. She didn't know if the persuasion she was about to attempt was a felony or a misdemeanor, but it certainly was daunting. She was the type who doesn't drive over 25 mph in a school zone.

Stalling, Tova asked irrelevant questions about allergies, smoking habits, and flossing methods, until she hit upon an idea.

She quickly scribbled her phone number on a scrap of paper and folded it. Tova then proceeded to do the job for which she was paid. When the examination was completed Tova requested in the most casual way that she could, "Would you mind giving me a call at home tonight?"

"Is there something wrong?" Svetlana asked in a panic.

"On the contrary," Tova assured her, "everything looks fine. It's a personal matter that I would like to discuss with you after hours." She pressed the piece of paper with her number into the lady's hand.

"Okay," Svetlana assured, regaining her composure.

"So you'll call me tonight?" Tova repeated, looking very intently into Svetlana's eyes.

"I promise," she vowed.

ALL NIGHT, Tova waited up for a phone call that never came. She moderately consoled herself that at least she had made an effort, but still a prick of angst gnawed at her conscience.

Two nights later, Svetlana phoned.

Tova gushed with gratitude for the call and then wasted no time explaining why she wished to speak with her outside of the work environs. She would have preferred breaking the ice with a few moments of small talk, but she could think of nothing trivial to say to this perfect stranger.

"Why do you wish to undergo an abortion?" Tova asked rather matter-of-factly.

"Because I cannot afford the expense of pregnancy and delivery," Svetlana answered, equally business-like.

Tova thought fast, suddenly remembering what a rabbi from the Woodside neighborhood had once told her — that he knows of at least 150 couples who are desperate for a child. She repeated the number 150 in her mind several times and concluded, "I'm covered." She then offered Svetlana a grandiose proposal in dollars and cents to avoid terminating the pregnancy.

It was an offer that was truly hard to refuse and the two worked out the financial details. The final arrangement provided for a monthly stipend and a huge grant at birth. Now, all Tova had left was the simple job of locating a sponsor to underwrite her commitment; one call to Woodside should handle that.

IT TURNED OUT that a lot more than just one phone call was involved. The figure of 150 was a slight exaggeration and, of the four or five actual couples who were eager to adopt a child, none would have been a good match.

This left Tova Katz with the responsibility of locating adoptive parents. Even more pressing, she had to come up with the first of the monthly stipend payments in two weeks. She certainly did not have the resources personally, as her husband learned in *kollel*.

For the next five months, until the Katzes succeeded in locating appropriate adoptive parents, Tova became a fund solicitor and talented magician in raising the monthly figure that she had committed to. Every month there was a miracle, usually at the very last white-knuckled second, to acquire the stipend figure.

To her own total incredulity, Tova honored her pledge down to the last penny. The intended adoptive parents lived in Lakewood, New Jersey, and they didn't blink at the arm and a leg that this baby would cost them. "How can you put a price on priceless?" they reasoned.

BENNY AND DEENA Isaacson had been undergoing exquisite suffering from their childless situation and there probably wasn't a worse place on earth to endure it. People like to say that Torah governs life in Lakewood, but the case could easily be made that children *dominate* life in Lakewood.

The streets are filled with them, the schools are bursting with them, and discussion is rife with them. Many signs in shuls, most signs in stores and the majority of local activities are designed for families with children. Lakewood may easily be the maternity capital of the world.

Salt on a wound is not a precise analogy for a barren couple in Lakewood. The situation is more akin to drying tender, sensitive skin with pink fiberglass insulation.

The plight of the Isaacsons was arguably among the worst, for most other couples in their boat and at their age had moved away from Lakewood. Their friends had already celebrated bar mitzvahs, and were contemplating which seminary to send their daughters. Both Benny and Deena came from moderately large families and each of their siblings had at least three children.

No matter where they went, they were haunted by their barrenness. If they were around those unaware of their straits, they were subjected to a barrage of grievances by those complaining about their blessing.

"Who do these babysitters think they are? They raise their price by a dollar just because they know you are desperate and then they expect you to be endlessly grateful to them."

"Anybody know anyone who wants a kid? Mine is ready for adoption. He has kept us up for two solid nights in a row and it's boiling down to either him or me."

"What were they thinking when they

set tuition fees? That we shouldn't have children?!"

"The pressure of *shidduchim* makes you wonder if it was all worth it. You raise a child for twenty years only to be rejected and ignored day after day."

Those aware of the Isaacsons' circumstances attempted to be sensitive, but it often backfired, causing some mortifying situations. They could always tell when a group of men or women were discussing children for as soon as either one of them approached, the conversation would abruptly end and a long stretch of awkward silence would descend.

Deena once happened upon her neighbor in the supermarket just as her children were undergoing a meltdown. The woman was simply unable to cope with all of the kids seeking their mother's attention at once. The baby was crying, two children inside the shopping cart were wailing hysterically, and a toddler was complaining loudly.

"May I help?" Deena offered, extending

her arms to accept the baby and free the mother's hands. Handing a baby to a fellow shopper is not an uncommon occurrence in a friendly community like Lakewood. The mother spun around, ready to hand over her bawling baby, but when she saw who her savior was she pulled the child back to her chest and lied, "I'm fine. Thank you anyway."

One Sunday morning, Benny caught up to some men who were emerging from shul. They were commenting over the ingenious prize that had been awarded to their sons at the *Avos U'vanim* learning session the night before. As soon as one of the fathers noticed Benny he sought to be considerate by dismissing, "The way the kids fight over these silly toys, I wish I didn't have to be involved in the whole thing!"

IN THE FIRST years that the Isaacsons were married, everyone thought that they were making their own generous contribution to rectify the situation by awarding them the *kvatter* honor at a bris. Over time both Benny and Deena came to view *kvatter* as nothing more than public humiliation. It was a smug joke and if someone were tasteless enough to offer it to them Benny would firmly decline, to prevent the significantly-his-junior *baal hasimcha* from arguing about "How much we always looked forward to giving you this honor" and "You are exactly the ones we had in mind" and "It would mean everything in the world if you would only accept to be *kvatter*," blah, blah, blah.

As the years advanced, people at family *s'machos* stopped wishing the Isaacsons, "*Im yirtzeh Hashem* by you," for fear that it would be viewed as a *brachah l'vatalah.*

The costs involved in their infertility treatments and workups were by no means negligible, weren't covered by insurance and had decimated the Isaacsons' finances. They were also physically painful. Yet the greatest burden was the emotional toll.

Month after month, expectations were raised only to be shattered. "Month after month" may not sound that disastrous, but it was also *year after year* for over a decade until Tova Katz made the connection and arranged the deal. All of Tova's efforts and turmoil were well worth the relief that this baby would afford the Isaacsons. She had found a loving and a deserving home for Svetlana's baby and relieved herself of further financial responsibility.

TO THE ISAACSONS, it was critically important that the baby be born on their turf. This was not a difficult request, and to spare Benny or Deena the awkwardness of driving in a car for four hours with the strange mother of their child, Tova's husband offered to make the trek. As it was the end of the month of Elul he claimed that he was eager to visit Lakewood and take in a *shmuz* in any event.

The day after Svetlana arrived in Lakewood, Tova received a most distressing call. It was Deena Isaacson on the line and she explained that Svetlana had undergone an ECHO exam which revealed that the baby was not well. This is not what they had been told, this is not what they had been promised, and the deal was off. As awkward as it was, they were preparing to drive Svetlana back to Silver Spring.

Tova was totally unprepared for this phone call. She had been feeling so good about her not-insignificant effort and now it was being rewarded with resentment. And where was she supposed to come up with $25,000? And... And, the whole situation was physiologically too much for her to bear as she was also in her ninth month and she feared that her aggravation would culminate in contractions.

Suddenly she stopped herself, calmed down and uttered in a tone devoid of self-pity, "I performed an ultrasound on Svetlana, and I am as good as any other technician out there. I didn't see any cause for concern and therefore you can trust me when I declare that there is *no* problem. If there is something that could have been picked up from an ultrasound, I would have noticed it."

The conviction of her words and the assuredness of her message turned the Isaacsons around instantaneously. They begged her apology and reset their minds to the rapidly approaching day when they would become parents.

Tova Katz finally released the breath she had been holding.

SVETLANA'S due date was the first day of Rosh Hashanah. For thirteen years, Benny had been the *baal tokei'ah* at his minyan and he was a central fixture of the davening. But this year he had begged a leave of absence as he wanted to be physically present when the baby was born. If this sounds a tad bizarre, that means that you are not looking at the situation from the perspectives of the over-a-decade-long-deprived Isaacsons.

Benny and Deena made arrangements with the hospital and that is where they spent the holiday, immersed as always, in sincere, intense prayer and supplications. The baby was not born on either day of Rosh Hashanah, but because the Isaacsons were serendipitously situated in the hospital, they were able to help out a significant number of people who would have otherwise been lost.

In the early afternoon of *Tzom Gedalyah*, the third day of the new year, a delightful, hirsute boy was born to Deena and Benny Isaacson. His bris was on Yom Kippur and despite the fast and the heat, the *simcha* was one of the most crowded affairs that even the old-time Lakewooders could re-member.

Since I reserved the right to tell this sto-ry in the first person, I resume my preroga-tive. It is at this point, when I tell this story, that I get choked up. It takes me back to when I was single and later as a newlywed, learning at the feet of Reb Shlomo Zalman *zt"l*.

Rav Auerbach loved people, and most of all he loved making people happy. Smiles are often contagious — and perhaps that is why he always wore one. Not long before he passed away, he blessed a young family member: "Learn well. Eat well. Sleep well. And always smile."

The Gaon had a special place in his heart for children and young people. He once said that he would not consider it beneath his dignity to be the traditional "candy man" in shul.

I can just imagine how happy Reb Sh-lomo Zalman would have been to learn of the Isaacsons' baby. He would have re-joiced with them from afar and smiled in the loving way that only he could.

IT ONCE HAPPENED that a wealthy individual, who apparently held himself in high esteem, came to visit Reb Shlomo Zalman. The philanthropist, immaculately attired, addressed the Gaon in a manner that matched his sartorial splendor.

"You are a highly respected personage," he said by way of greeting. "It is therefore beyond my comprehension that you should involve yourself with the multitude of intricacies relevant to the subject of infertility. It is simply inappropriate for an individual of your stature."

Reb Shlomo Zalman asked his guest to clarify his objection. The Rav assumed that his distinguished detractor wished to challenge the halachic validity of his numerous dispensations, and would attempt to prove that they were not halachically sound.

But this man's objections lay neither in the realm of Torah nor in medical expertise. Rather, he felt that it was undignified for a *talmid chacham* of Reb Shlomo Zalman's standing to concern himself with an issue relating to *women*.

After hearing the nature of the objection, Reb Shlomo Zalman asked the individual how many children he had.

"Six," he replied proudly.

"Are you not ashamed of yourself?" the Gaon demanded. "You and your wife have, thank God, six children, while there are many couples who have none. May you never know the suffering of these couples whose anguish is so great and whose misery is so keen. I see nothing inappropriate about dealing with their plight, and with God's help, perhaps relieving it. The subject is too vital to be left only to others. For me it is both a duty and an honor."

AS I WRITE THESE WORDS, my eyes begin to swim, for this is clearly the sequel to the Karen Classic. Even from high above in *Shomayim,* Reb Shlomo Zalman Auerbach is still lobbying and affecting our People. His personal imprint is on the whole story. And those warm, moist eyes I'm sure are also looking down on the Isaacson family and smiling in the loving way that was his alone.

❃

AND, before I forget, two weeks later, Tova gave birth to a baby. Naturally, she named him Shlomo Zalman after the man who had given her the greatest gift she could have ever hoped for: the privilege of saving a life and of providing a formerly heavyhearted couple with constant smiles.

Heard from: Rivka Grumet

Home Coming

*N*ATIONS, LIKE SO many living organisms, are often born in blood.

The modern state of Israel is no exception. Those who fought and died came from the broadest possible array of backgrounds, but they shared a single dream: to return to their ancestral land as free men. To the great rabbinic sages of the day (the Chofetz Chaim most prominent among them), that dream was articulated in a powerful formula for a strong and purposeful Jewish homeland: *"The land is the body of Israel... but the Torah is its soul."* And both body and soul are essential, in order for the fledgling entity to fulfill its spiritual mission in the world.

A young army and an ancient Torah, blood and hope, time and distance and destiny: this is the collage embodied by a faded newspaper photo taken on the 25th of July, 1949, in the 4,000-year-old port of Tel Aviv/Jaffa. Rabbis and soldiers, dignitaries and civilians cheer and weep on the dock, as the ship's blond-haired captain (a shiny black *kippah* perched awkwardly on his head) directs the unloading of a most precious cargo...

FOLLOWING Israel's War of Independence, its various military organizations (Palmach, Ezel and Lechi) were all incorporated into one, to be known from that day forward as the Israel Defense Forces. Incorporation, however, did not mean cohesion. Even a common enemy and a common military purpose were not enough to bridge the gap between soldiers from vastly different cultures and religious upbringings.

Initially, separate units were created for religiously observant soldiers, with kosher food and other spiritual accommodations, to minimize the costs to the nascent (and financially-strapped) IDF. This was also a method to avert accusations from the Left of "religious coercion" in Israel's armed forces.

Nevertheless, there were unforeseen problems. Casualties within these religious units were devastating to Israel's tightly knit religious community, where everyone knew everyone else. Each loss on the battle-field became a disaster on the home front as well, deeply ravaging morale. These pla-toons also represented a violation of a key tenet of Ben Gurion's policy: that there would be but one united procedure for the new state in general, and its armed forces in particular.

Enter Plan B. Under the new direc-tive, observant soldiers would be distrib-uted throughout the various divisions and ranks of the IDF, and their religious needs would be met as a matter of national gen-eral policy. Shabbos observance, the prepa-ration and distribution of kosher food, and the establishment of a synagogue on every base became standard operating procedure. To execute and oversee these initiatives, the Military Rabbinate was launched, increased numbers of religious soldiers were inducted, and the IDF's religious programs and accommodations steadily expanded.

Except one. There were not enough Torah scrolls to go around.

Not enough Torahs for the new base synagogues — and not enough, either, in the rest of Israel, with its influx of refugees from war-torn Europe and Arab countries alike. Many of these survivors hailed from vibrant centers of European Jewish life where exquisitely bedecked *sifrei Torah* had once abounded. But these holy scrolls — like the great shuls and tiny *shtieblach* that housed them, and the faithful Jews who so treasured them — had all gone up in smoke.

So how does a nation find its Torahs?

Where does a body find its soul?

THE ANSWER, most unexpectedly, came from the halls of academia. At the 30-year-

old Hebrew University of Jerusalem, a
young immigrant named Meir Sompolinsky was completing his graduate work
in Jewish history, with an emphasis upon
the Jews of Denmark, his country of origin. Through his studies, Meir had discovered that only during the 20th century
had Denmark's Jewish life become central-
ized in Copenhagen; for generations prior,
smaller enclaves had dotted the country's
map.

What had become of all the religious artifacts from these forgotten communities?
According to Meir's research, the last available documentation was of removal to a
storehouse in Copenhagen. *Could they,* he
wondered, *be there still?*

In April of 1949, ten months after the
establishment of the Jewish State, Meir
Sompolinsky convinced the head of Israel's
Defense Ministry to authorize him to find
out, and he flew back to Copenhagen.

There was reason to believe — to hope
— that these artifacts might have actually
survived the conflagration. Denmark's Jewish community was the only one that was

largely spared in the Holocaust. This particular chapter of history Meir did not glean
from a book; it was the story of the family
he had left behind.

Germany never occupied its northern
neighbor the way it conquered other countries, for strictly strategic reasons. Denmark
had a bountiful and efficiently-run food
supply system that the Germans considered
a crucial asset, believing as they did, that
it was not military defeat but widespread
hunger both in the military ranks and the
civilian population, that brought them to
their knees in World War I. Because of this
sensitivity to the problem of provisions,
the Nazis permitted the Danes to maintain
their democratic authority even after the
incursion.

The government in Denmark afforded
significant autonomy to all Danish citizens
including the Jews. This was not the German intention, but the Danes — from King
Christian X on down — demonstrated a no-
tolerance policy on systematic persecution
of the Jews. Virulent, local anti-Semitism
— key to the successful implementation
of the Final Solution throughout Europe

— was defiantly *un*characteristic of Denmark.

Even those Danes who hadn't seen it with their own eyes were aware that every morning their King, Christian X, rode his horse through the heart of the city to strengthen his bonds with his people. Because he refused bodyguards, and the animosity between the king and the Nazis was so well known, hundreds of Danes rode alongside him on their bicycles, surrounding him like human shields. His route took him past the Machzikei Hadass synagogue, and the worshippers, just emerging from *Shacharis*, would stand at attention as one of them recited the blessing for a monarch. The king never failed to be touched and would salute in response.

On September 26th, 1942, when King Christian X's birthday was celebrated as a national holiday, congratulatory telegrams poured in from all over the world. Hitler's greeting was unusual in its length, politesse and effusive good wishes. The king's reply was remarkably unusual in its brevity: "Thanks. Christian X."

Hitler was not one to be snubbed. He ordered a number of measures to punish the king and his people, but the Danes staunchly rallied around their monarch. At the same time, seismic shifts were occurring in the military theater. For in the final months of 1942, the British defeated the Germans and the Italians in Libya, removing the Nazi threat to the Middle East; and the Russian army had turned the tide in Stalingrad, placing Germany on the defensive for the first time. Clandestine anti-Nazi activity throughout Denmark surged.

Every action brings about a reaction; and every reaction, a stronger counter reaction. As underground groups escalated their attacks against German soldiers and interests, the Danish king was placed under house arrest, the Danish army was stripped of its weapons, and hundreds of prominent Danes — including the Chief Rabbi, his son and the *gabba'im* of the Great Synagogue — were sent to a detention camp outside Copenhagen. At the time of these arrests, the Gestapo impounded the Jewish communal lists — an ominous sign for Danish Jewry. Alas, the leadership of the Jewish community did not issue a public alert, leaving the

Jews of Denmark in the same peril as the rest of European Jewry.

Meir Sompolinsky had left Denmark for Israel before the darkness fell. But many of his countrymen, including members of his own family, were not as fortunate.

IN LATE SEPTEMBER, 1943, two mysterious German cargo ships docked in the Copenhagen harbor. George Dukowitz, the German attaché for shipping in Denmark, risked his career — indeed, his life — to leak the true purpose of the ships to Danish government officials, who quickly informed the leaders of the Jewish community...who once again failed to act responsibly. The cargo ships had been designated to deport Danish Jewry to extermination camps. But instead of notifying everyone to flee, the so-called leaders focused solely on their own escape, locking all the communal funds in a bank vault with strict instructions forbidding its removal. This act alone cost precious lives, as it prevented access to monies that could have gone to rescue efforts.

The captives were to be taken by surprise and rounded up in their homes on Rosh

Hashanah, the very last day of September, courtesy of the lists recently impounded by the Nazis.

Into the shameful vacuum of communal and rabbinic leadership stepped Danes from every walk of life — beginning with King Christian X himself. While still under house arrest, he wrote a stinging letter condemning the impending expulsion, which made its way all the way up to the Foreign Ministry in Berlin.

On the streets of Copenhagen, or riding the streetcars, Jews were startled by offers of keys to apartments and cottages from complete strangers as places to hide.

Mendel Katlev, a Jewish foreman in a leather-goods factory, heard at work of the planned round-up and immediately boarded the next train home. The conductor, who regularly saw Katlev, even though the two had never spoken, casually asked him why he had departed from his usual schedule. When Katlev revealed that he was rushing home to seek a hiding-place for his family, the conductor — without a moment's hesitation — offered them refuge.

An ambulance driver named Jorgen Knudsen pored over local telephone directories, copying down the "Jewish-sounding" names. He then visited every address he had recorded to warn of the incipient danger. If someone told him they had nowhere to escape to, he would drive them in his ambulance to the Bispebjerg Hospital, where they would be hidden inside the wards.

And as Rosh Hashanah drew near, the good citizens of Copenhagen frantically raced to inform their Jewish neighbors to run for their lives. If not for the persistence of those who sounded the alarm, most of the synagogues would have conducted services as usual; instead, their doors were bolted shut.

Denmark's Jews had their own Paul Revere in the person of Dovid Sompolinsky, Meir's brother. Drafted into the Danish Army in 1942 and subsequently assigned to the National Guard, Dovid wore police officer's attire and had all the privileges of a man in blue.

Every advantage, every connection, and

every ounce of cunning he possessed, he marshaled on behalf of his brethren on the eve of Rosh Hashanah.

Bursting into one spacious house to alert its residents, Dovid was stunned to find 30 families gathered in secret for prayers. He quickly summoned a doctor, who diagnosed all those present with a rare and highly contagious disease. Rushed by ambulance to a local hospital, they were hastened into quarantine — along with the *sefer Torah*, shofar, and *talleisim* that would have been the nails in their coffins...

One by one, the Jews of Denmark finally began to understand the gravity of their situation. But the elderly and the infirm were in no position to take action. The patriarchs and matriarchs of Danish Jewry, hundreds of souls, seemed destined for the flames.

With only a rickety bicycle to rely on, Dovid Sompolinsky pedaled himself frantically to Copenhagen's municipal home for the elderly and, with a bravado matching his uniform, commanded its director to prepare for an influx of hundreds of new residents. The urgency of the policeman was lost on this individual, who calmly agreed to admit them... provided that he also got a bank check that would cover the costs.

Dovid hopped back on his bike, this time to the private bank where the *kehilla*'s account was held. But the Jewish manager had already fled, and the Christian employees had strict orders to deny access to the account. These funds, had they only been available, could easily have compensated Swedish fisherman to transport Jews out of Denmark, under cover of night...

IN THE MEANTIME, the SS, with their characteristic, chilling efficiency, lost no time in swooping down upon the Jewish old-age home. One of the residents being expelled was widely recognized, at age 101, as the oldest living woman in the Danish kingdom. The brutality with which she was treated so outraged the Danes who witnessed it, that the Germans had no recourse but to carry her back to her room. Other seniors, however, were taken by force to the synagogue and grilled mercilessly about covert sabotage operations. Their pleas of complete ignorance were met with savage beatings.

Dovid Sompolinsky tirelessly attempted every possible avenue of rescue, and a few impossible ones. His desperate journey ultimately brought him to the steps of his former high school, the Christianshavns Gymnasium. Here he discovered a hotbed of underground anti-Nazi operations. The school's principal, Frederik Boegh, had rallied his teachers to the cause; as most of them lived in the "Kongens Lyngby" district (adjacent to the royal palace where Christian X remained under arrest). They — and the students who joined their efforts — became known as the "Lyngby Group."

Working with the Lyngby Group was, for Dovid, a dizzying crash course in risk management. One of the organization's greatest challenges was providing adequate nutrition for the Jews they had placed in hiding, especially the children. Dovid turned for help to the head pharmacist in the hospital where his reserve unit was stationed, who invited Dovid to his home — in Lyngby, as it happened — where he had a sizeable stash of vitamins, considered contraband in wartime. But soon after arriving there, Dovid received word of a new group of refugees who needed to be hidden at once.

In matters of life and death, liberties are taken. Dovid had traveled to the pharmacist's home by train, but in his haste to depart, he jumped aboard an unlocked bicycle he spotted leaning against a railing outside. When he returned several hours later, after completing his mission, he came face-to-face with the bike's enraged owner, a teacher, who demanded an explanation from the thief in uniform. It took some doing, but the raw power of Dovid Sompolinsky's explanation rocked Aage Bertelsen's world. From this rocky beginning, a crucial alliance was forged.

And on that fateful Rosh Hashanah, hundreds of Danish Jews were hidden inside the homes of the Lyngby Group, Aage Bertelsen's home among them. A secret code was developed by the teachers, using construction terms to convey information about the terrified souls harbored within their walls. They spoke offhandedly about concrete and two-by-fours, hammers and screws, plaster and paint. Only they knew that these words referred to flesh-and-blood, not sticks of wood; that their concern was not the foundation of a building but the very foundation of humanity itself: the courage to do right in the face of monstrous injustice.

ON THE DAY of the great round-up, the Nazis succeeded in capturing only 284 men, women and children, the majority seized from the Jewish old-age home. More than 7,000 — by the grace of God and good neighbors — were oddly unaccounted for.

Even so, an effective escape route was still needed for Danish Jewry. And thus the greatest secret rescue operation of WWII was launched: a collaborative venture between the Danish underground and a group of Swedish fisherman, who, for a tidy sum (understandable, due to the enormous risks involved), smuggled the remainder of Denmark's Jews into neutral Sweden.

Once again, the courageous members of the Lyngby Group played a key role: hiding the fugitives, arranging for the boats, and paying off the fisherman in the event that individuals did not have adequate funds of their own for their "passage." Aage Bertelsen routinely "borrowed" money from his affluent associates, pledging to repay at the war's end. One wealthy log merchant, overwhelmed by the opportunity to save innocent lives, presented Bertelsen, without any hesitation or fanfare, the equivalent of half a million dollars.

While the size of the bequest was unusual, the generosity behind it was emblematic of what was happening throughout the country of Denmark. Ephraim Sompolinsky, another brother to Dovid and Meir, was once approached by an unknown gentleman on a streetcar, who gave him the heavily lined winter coat right off his back. "Here," he said, pressing the coat into Ephraim's hands. "You'll be needing this where you are headed."

Dovid, too, had benefited from the kindness of strangers. He was on foot one day when a bicyclist accosted him, warning that the Gestapo were in the area making arrests; he insisted that Dovid take his bicycle, which he did — to the nearest hospital, where, once again, a phalanx of compassionate doctors and nurses quickly quarantined him with some "dreaded disease."

Between Rosh Hashanah and Simchas Torah, 1943, 7,220 Danish Jews were safely evacuated to Sweden, 1,000 of them via the Lyngby Group. In addition, the Danish government never gave up on the 480 Danish Jews who were deported to the Theresienstadt concentration camp, periodically sending them shipments of food and clothing. When the Danes insisted that a Red Cross delegation visit the prisoners, the Nazis agreed, if only as a most outrageous propaganda charade. At the war's end, however, the Danes employed manipulations of their own when the camp's authorities refused to release Danish survivors onto Red Cross busses bound for Sweden — convincing them to reverse their decree by dangling premium cuts of pork and fine whiskey before their hungry eyes.

IT WAS NO WONDER, then, that the solemn search for the only Torahs to survive the scourge of World War II, would focus on the proud country of Denmark.

Meir Sompolinsky was warmly welcomed as a returning son of Denmark, the moment he set foot upon its soil. The Great Synagogue of Copenhagen had a newly appointed rabbi whose son and daughter were volunteers in the fledgling Israeli army. This august congregation elected to donate no fewer than 31 *sifrei Torah* to the IDF! The much smaller Machzikei Hadass synagogue dipped into their lesser reserve to contribute eight of their precious scrolls. And a third shul, founded by a faction that had broken away from the main synagogue some years earlier, sought at last to be reunited with the rest of *klall Yisrael* by donating three of their Torahs.

Meir vaguely remembered from his youth that the Jewish tailors of Copenhagen — a dominant presence in the community — also had their own *minyan*. The *"Schneider Shtiebel"* ("Tailors' Prayer-hall") had disbanded, but where could their Torah scroll have gone? By asking the right questions, he found his way to a storage closet inside the Machzikei Hadass synagogue. There, the last surviving member of the *Schneider Shtiebel* was summoned, and he graciously agreed that their *sefer Torah* should have an "aliyah" to Israel.

The exhilarating successes of this first leg of Meir's journey inspired him to push on. From Copenhagen, he traveled north to Malmoe, Sweden, a community that donated two of its *sifrei Torah*, and more were added by the tiny Jewish communities of Helsingborg and Goetenborg.

Mitzvah begat mitzvah, miracle begat miracle, as Meir Sompolinsky continued in his quest. And yet the greatest treasure to be mined — a rumored stockpile of *sifrei Torah* in Stockholm — had a murky past. A Swedish Jew was the sole owner of the scrolls, having acquired them (sometime during the 1920s or '30s) from Soviet profiteers, after Communism put a chokehold on all manifestations of religious expression. He went ahead with this purchase in defiance of a rabbinic ban against stripping Russian Jewry of the precious few ritual objects they still had. In response, the synagogues of Sweden refused to allow these "contraband" *sifrei Torah* into their holy arks.

To resolve his quandary about the appropriateness of hunting down all these

Torahs, Meir turned to Rabbi Shlomo Goren, chief rabbi of the IDF, for a ruling. Rabbi
Goren proclaimed that every effort should
be made to redeem the scrolls by bringing
them to the Holy Land, where they would
finally be used again. But despite this ruling and Meir's subsequent entreaties, the
Swede refused to relinquish his purchase.*

---

* A bewildering epilogue occurred several months
later. The son of the purchaser from the Commu-
nists, his face framed with the unshaven beard of a
mourner, arrived in Israel equipped with a *sefer Torah*. He made his way to Sompolinsky and conveyed
that he wished to donate this *sefer* of his father's,
who had recently passed away, to a synagogue in
Israel; he was totally mute about the fate of the others.

Meir saw to it that this *sefer Torah* would be admitted to its new home with adequate fanfare and
the chief *Sefaradi chazzan* of Tel Aviv conducted the
festivities. Alas, the first time this *sefer Torah* was
read from it was found to be faulty. An expert *sofer*
was summoned and he spent days repairing the entire *sefer*. But even after this, every time the scroll
was read from new problems crept up. In due time it
was removed from the cycle of regular reading.

The prevailing sense was that since this holy
scroll had been acquired in violation of the rabbinic
ban, the scroll was not blessed. Hence, reading from
the *sefer* was no longer an option and it is only used
on *simchas Torah* when it is danced with (serving

STUNG, yet undeterred by this singular rejection, Meir next set his sights on the Finnish capital of Helsinki. There, the Jewish community immediately donated five Torahs from its modest collection. Meir's gratitude for their extreme generosity was tarnished only by his disappointment that none of the Torahs was one of the rare, miniature *sifrei Torah* described by historians.

Helsinki's Jewish community was nonexistent until the nineteenth century, when it grew slowly around a core group of released Cantonists, Jewish youths who had been forcibly inducted into the Russian army via state-sponsored, mass kidnappings. Ostensibly designed to fill the quota of Jews in the Czar's army, the *real* motive of these abductions was to rob the young soldiers of all ties to Judaism. The plan, by all accounts, seemed to work.

But after the Cantonists had completed their term of twenty-five years in the garrisons of Helsinki, the Russian authorities

---

simultaneously as a poignant reminder of a tragic period in Jewish history).

permitted them to remain in frigid Finland. These clandestine Jews hired scribes to write miniature *sifrei Torah* that could easily be concealed inside a military backpack. Meir was eager to unearth these tiny gems for use by IDF units in the field. But the *gabbaoim* of the Helsinki synagogue had no idea what had become of them.

Meir believed his Scandinavian adventure had come to an end, when he received a surprise invitation from the Jewish leadership of Turku, a tiny, remote enclave in western Finland. "It would mean everything to us," they wrote enthusiastically, "to host a guest from Israel."

Who could refuse such a heartfelt request? Upon his arrival, Meir was impressed not only by the community's warmth, but by its knowledge of Judaism, the last thing he had expected in such a far-flung outpost. He was surprised to discover that, prior to the war, a number of their townsmen had crossed the Baltic Gulf to learn in the legendary *yeshivos* of Lithuania, and returned to share their spiritual wealth.

Meir mentioned his hope of acquiring

one of the rare mini-Torahs but only one of the *gabba'im*, a very elderly man, dimly recalled ever having seen such a treasure in their shul, decades earlier. Notwithstanding, they assured their guest that they, too, wished to present a *sefer Torah* to the defenders of the Jewish State, steering him to their shul's ornate *aron kodesh* to assist in its selection.

Meir had run across a variety of arresting *aronot kodesh* during his travels, but the Turku synagogue's ark was jaw-droppingly one-of-a-kind. It contained a mechanical apparatus (designed by a long-ago rabbi, custom-built by a carpenter) whose gears rotated the *sifrei Torah* on a circular platform, guaranteeing that no scroll was "disrespected" by being left out of the reading cycle, or was deprived of proper maintenance.

Meir was so caught up by the ingenuity of the system, the proud *gabba'im* decided to really show it off. They set the contraption to its highest speed, setting the platform awhirl in a spinning carousel of Torahs. Suddenly, dislodged by the centrifugal force, a miniature *sefer Torah* came flying out — and, amidst a chorus of gasps, was safely caught!

When they got over the shock, they all agreed: this was destiny. The tiny, amazingly portable Torah would be a source of comfort and light to Jewish soldiers in the field. The community earmarked three additional full-sized scrolls to accompany their baby brother to the land of Israel.

MEIR SOMPOLINSKY returned to Copenhagen with 16 more *sifrei Torah* in his possession. The little Machzikei Hadass synagogue gave their eight Torahs a big send-off, hosting a gala celebration attended by strands of the community that were seldom united. And the following Shabbos, in the Great Synagogue, there was pomp and circumstance and much jubilation. All 31 *sifrei Torah* that this shul was donating, were marched around the sanctuary in a procession led by the guest of honor: Meir Sompolinsky, outfitted in an elegant top hat in the tradition of the *gabba'im* of Copenhagen.

It was the first of Iyar — one year since the establishment of the State of Israel —

the week of its first Independence Day. In his address the Rabbi reminded the congregation how just one year prior, they had collected money for arms, and how blessed it was that on this day they were providing Torah scrolls to the very same army.

Zvi Margolinsky, who in October of 1943 had risked life and limb to transport dozens of Torah scrolls (on his bicycle, no less) to their secret hiding place inside a Copenhagen church, now had the honor of personally bringing them, under a bright sun, to the Sompolinsky's apartment, in joyful anticipation of their passage.

BUT there were miles — oceans — to go, before Meir could sleep. Never did he conceive of a mandate to ship *59 sifrei Torah!* The Ministry of Defense had no budget to finance such an operation, and the various transport agencies Meir urgently contacted one after the other showed little-to-no interest in underwriting this momentous *mitzvah.*

Once again, Meir wrestled with a dilemma both practical and existential:

How does a nation bring home its Torahs?

How does a body unite with its soul?

This time, the answer emanated from the chambers of the human heart. Meir learned that a vessel belonging to a Dutch shipping company would soon have a port call in Copenhagen en route to Tel Aviv. He rushed to the headquarters of the company's agent, where a helpful young clerk proceeded to ask him all of the standard questions — and get none of the standard answers.

Instead of diving into a brisk recitation of weights and measurements, shipping dates and customs details and bills of lading, Meir Sompolinsky waded slowly through a tale of armies and Torahs, blood and hope, time and distance and destiny. He spoke of men with serial numbers branded into their forearms who were now proud soldiers; of women whose babies had been brutally wrestled from their arms, gathering strength to have more babies; of children who breathed the air of freedom for the very first time. He spoke of an unapologetic king on a horse, of good people who helped neighbors without thought to the consequences. He spoke of 59 scrolls, collected across thousands of miles, that now stood waiting in his parents' apartment, because he had no money to bring them... home. He spoke of a newborn nation — a body that was ready to be united with its soul.

The clerk, his eyes awash with tears, sent a telegram to the head office in Amsterdam. The response was swift. The 59 *sifrei Torah* would be shipped at no charge, and Meir's father would accompany them on their journey, as a first-class passenger and personal guest of the captain.

The voyage of the 59 Torahs took just four days — a blink of an eye, really, in the long sweep of history. As he watched the ship's captain direct the unloading of his most precious cargo Meir Sompolinsky could only smile, recalling the closing message of the Chief Rabbi of Copenhagen as the Torahs had made their final *"hakafos"* around the sanctuary of the Great Synagogue. "From Copenhagen shall go forth Torah," the rabbi had declared, "and the word of the Lord from Jerusalem!"

Under the newsman's lens, that morning of 25th of July, 1949, time and distance and destiny were reuniting the Land of Israel with its Torah soul.

Meir Sompolinsky completed his mission of redeeming 59 *sifrei Torah* from a dingy warehouse and other venues of disuse on the fourth of Iyar, 1949. *Fifty-nine years later, on the fourth of Iyar* — Memorial Day for the IDF's fallen soldiers, those for whom Meir extended himself — his soul was returned to its maker.

Based on: Echad Min Ha'ir by Meir Sompolinsky

Cherished

Pure Love

*H*OW DID he do it?

How did one man fulfill his destiny, reach the pinnacle of success in his chosen field, even alter the course of history... with almost *none* of the tools that the modern world deems essential?

It's all about "who you know" — but Rabbi Shraga Feivel Mendlowitz arrived on American shores in 1913 without knowing a single soul.

You've got to have a support system... but he came alone, leaving his family and his associates behind in Hungary.

Communication is everything, but his English was broken.

Credentials are critical — and he had possessed an outstanding one, *semichah* from three of Hungary's *gedolim* — but he adamantly refused to call himself (or to let anybody else call him) "Rabbi."

Nobody likes a quitter, but he quit the career he originally trained for — working as a *shochet* — the very first day on the job.

Only the strong survive, but he was often unwell, with a painful ulcer aggravated by the fact that he was unable to afford proper nutrition or medical care.

Money makes the world go 'round... — but he managed to launch and "grow" a national educational movement with almost no resources.

RABBI S. F. MENDLOWITZ (1886-1948) was the visionary and architect of Torah education as we know it today. As we look around at the proliferation of Jewish day schools throughout the U.S., it is hard to believe that seventy-five years ago, such institutions did not even exist — and that an unassuming immigrant was the catalyst for nothing less than a seismic shift in Jewish learning, that will reverberate for generations.

How did he do it? I've often asked myself. *What was his secret?*

I recently stumbled upon a never-before revealed story — a brilliant little gem, really, too beautiful not to share — that sheds light upon the bigger picture.

But first, a bit more about Rabbi Mendlowitz. Or *Mr.* Mendlowitz, as he insisted upon being called.

His first destination in the U.S. was New York's Lower East Side. His heart was never in the *shechitah* business; this he knew the very first time he stood on his own, with a shuddering fowl in his grasp, no longer a student or an apprentice-*shochet* but the prime wielder of the sharp blade. Shraga

Feivel understood, then and there, that he was destined to *add* to — not take away from — life.

HIS NEXT STOP was Scranton, Pennsylvania, which had a sizeable enclave of Hungarian Jews. His lifelong dream was to establish a yeshivah, to teach and mentor and inspire others as he had been taught, mentored and inspired. But this lofty idea appeared pie-in-the-sky, in an era and an America marked by dizzying social, political and technological change, and a fixation on all that was modern. So the dream remained a dream, and the young Rabbi's pedagogic outlet became teaching "Hebrew school" classes to the youth of Scranton. The children were, for the most part, spent and unruly after a full day in public school, and preferred to spend their afternoons fraternizing or playing ball.

Reb Shraga Feivel understood that his efforts were futile, and he tendered his resignation every single day of his first three weeks in Scranton. The president of the community refused to accept it, declaring his strong faith in the young *melamed*. (Read: he had no replacement.)

So Reb Shraga Feivel soldiered on. Nearly all of his meager salary went to room and board — though it wasn't much of a room, and for one who stringently upheld the laws of *kashrus,* the diet was so severely limited that it eroded his health.

Although he was indisputably the town's *melamed,* he never even hinted at his prestigious *semichah,* acquired from the Unsdorfer Rav. When his hostess discovered his ordination certificate while cleaning for *Pesach*, Reb Shraga Feivel unceremoniously tore up the document and then burned the evidence.

It would be fair to say that Reb Shraga Feivel rebelled against the title of "rabbi" — but it was not without a cause. It was his personal protest against indiscriminate use of the title in America, as an honorific bestowed upon unworthy candidates and a remonstration against a rabbinate in America that was, by all appearances, sadly ineffective.

He also likely assumed that he would be more successful with the young if no title was affixed to his name; and finally, felt himself undeserving of the same appellation as the renowned scholars that he revered.

So "Mr. Mendlowitz" it was. In fact, callers seeking Rabbi Mendlowitz would be informed: "No one by that name lives here..."

After World War I, Reb Shraga Feivel finally managed to bring his wife and children to America, with assurances that they were headed for *Eretz Yisrael* with a stop in America along the way. He had good reason to be disillusioned with this country and to fulfill his pledge to his wife — but his dream burned within him; neither grinding poverty (his) nor utter complacency (American Jewry's) reduced the flame.

SO BACK TO THE QUESTION: How did he go from such modest beginnings — from zero — to transforming Mesivta Torah Vodaas into a world-class yeshivah, the gold standard for classical Jewish learning in a modern age, and create a new day school template that gave rise to hundreds of institutions modeled after it?

Let us add another question: How, back in 1944, did he grasp that bestowing the decidedly non-threatening title of "day school" upon this new venture, would make it palatable to American Jewry? It is stunning to contemplate that until that time in mid-twentieth century America, a bar mitzvah signified *the end of every child's Jewish learning forever,* except for those from the most religious families.

Today, the burgeoning day school movement is comprised of more than two-hundred schools, and almost a quarter-of-a-million students.

Clearly, he was a leader possessing out-standing attributes: a brilliant mind, a magnetic personality, rare sincerity and an unquenchable sense of mission. All these are important ingredients, to be sure, in the recipe for success. But there is one more, and *this*, I propose, is the one that "Mr." Shraga Feivel Mendlowitz possessed in abundance, and tended with every fiber of his being.

It was love. Passionate, pure, unadul-terated, egoless, selfless, unconditional, infinite — this was the love that Reb Shraga Feivel heaped upon the Almighty.

"Love" is a word used so indiscriminately in today's world that it has lost much of its power and meaning. But not Reb Shraga Feivel's love. His every thought and action was for the glory of *Hashem*; and their relationship was a two-way street.

Have we forgotten that spiritual success requires spiritual assistance?

A DISCIPLE of the rabbi's recently revealed this story:

During his early years in America, Reb Shraga Feivel could not afford to purchase a ticket to the synagogue for the *Yomim Noraim*. Seats had to be paid for in advance; there were no exceptions. It was a modest sum, but even this was beyond Reb Shraga Feivel's means — so a friend placed a stool for him underneath a set of dank stairs.

This pious Torah scholar, who would be recognized as one of the towering greats of American Jewry, was relegated to a confined, humid, mildewed corner where he could not sit erect. The man was penniless, alone, frustrated by failure, hampered by hardships, and consumed by an impossible dream. He certainly had plenty to pray for, to petition for.

But Reb Shraga Feivel's supplications were guided not by need; they were guided by love. He later confided to a disciple: "Although I didn't have a crumb of bread, a roof over my head, or any material thing to call my own, I did have prayer. And I prayed as devoutly as I could for but *one* thing: *that God's honor would be magnified and increased.*"

Reb Shraga Feivel Mendlowitz became the very agent by which his own prayer was fulfilled. As his name and his accomplishments and his teachings and his influence flourished, there was a palpable sense that *God wants this man to succeed.* And there's not a day-school-educated boy or girl, man or woman in America, who does not owe him a lifetime of gratitude.

How did he do it? This irksome question has now been answered.

How can *we* do it? This, each one of us must answer for ourselves.

Heard from: Rabbi Yaakov Leshinsky and based on *Shelucha DeRachmana* by Rabbi Aharon Sorasky

Words Worth

*F*AR BE IT from you, my brothers and sisters, the harrowing experience I am about to relate. It is every driver's nightmare, especially if you are Jewish, slight, and frightened of bad neighborhoods — and even more so if you drive a jalopy and are sent after dark to a slum so depressed that it is no longer even gallantly referred to as "Apache Territory." And this, just two days after riots and looting plagued every New York district but this one.

When the New York City Blackout hit

on July 13, 1977, the only area that was not affected was the Rockaways, as they were powered by the (now defunct) Long Island Lighting Company system. Every other district of the city, served by Con Edison, was thrust into both darkness and a rampage of vandalism and looting. Greedy, ransacking mobs descended upon stores and commercial enterprises to make off with whatever they could.

Thieves stole fifty new Pontiacs from a Bronx automotive dealership, and in Brooklyn, stores' grates were torn off by cars, enabling couches, televisions, and heaps of clothing to be paraded through the streets by looters who were at once defiant, furtive and gleeful. In several sections of Manhattan, you could hear the rumble of iron shutters being forced up and the shattering of storefront glass, followed by the emptying of electronics stores. Free access to DJ equipment turned Hip Hop dancing, barely known outside of the Bronx, into an overnight citywide — and subsequently nationwide — sensation. For the participants in the mayhem, it was a party, and many of the residents of the Rockaways were seething at being deprived of the spoils.

There were other factors that made this a less-than-opportune time for Shaindy Berkowitz to venture into a neighborhood that — even in the best of times, and in broad daylight — was the country's capital for illegal weapons and knifings per *hour*. Gunshots in the Rockaways were as frequently heard as sirens in the rest of the City.

That summer, one had the palpable sensation of being in a pressure cooker, as a brutal heat wave cooked the city from the beginning of July. At the same time, residents were fretting over the Son of Sam murders, and virtually everyone was suffering from a protracted economic downturn.

Meanwhile, Shaindy, wearing a pair of oversized glasses that made her look like a character out of an entry-level art sketchbook and exuding a naive wholesomeness and frothy effervescence that made her the original happy camper, was being coerced by her mother to run a little errand in the baddest part of the bad Rockaways. "I don't think it's such a good idea," Shaindy meekly pointed out. Her understated editorial comment was like Mussolini admitting he has a shouting problem.

"There is no point in your shlepping all the way out to the Island," Shaindy's mother pronounced, eighty-sixing her daughter's protest, "when the drugstore over there carries what I need."

Shaindy's nature was not to whine or beg, and she usually conceded to other people's suggestions of how to spend her time. In fact, that's how she got involved in visiting the nursing home.

SHAINDY'S OLDER SISTER and her friend used to visit the West Lawrence Care Center on Seagirt Boulevard in Far Rockaway, but they soon realized that there were just too many residents for the two of them to befriend on their own. One way to bolster their numbers by fifty percent was to induct Shaindy; and never was there an easier recruit. Once she started, she quickly grew to love her senior "hosts" — and her pleasant, cheerful demeanor endeared her to both residents and staff alike.

But trudging to a nursing home on Shabbos and driving to "Gun Central" on a Wednesday night weren't the same thing, and Shaindy's sense of self-preservation rendered her a tad more vocal than usual. "Wouldn't prudence be advisable over convenience?" she asked deferentially. But Mrs. Berkowitz was confident that her daughter would be back in no time, so there was nothing to fear.

The Berkowitzes were the none-too-proud owners of a circa 1964 Country Squire station wagon whose imitation-wood trim on the doors and tailgate looked like it had been devoured, in part, by starved, collossal termites. The sides were rust-corroded and the dash was an uneven ridge of cracked and peeling vinyl looking as if had been dislodged from the surface of Mercury. Due to the fragile connection between roof and car body, the buffeting noise at cruising speeds was reminiscent of a tent on a cliff in a hurricane.

WITH GREAT trepidation, Shaindy headed off for Mug City. As she descended into the entrails of the "'hood" her senses were assaulted by the open sewers, petrochemical cloud layers and every other olfactory offense indigenous to a slum. Surrounded by the frightful pandemonium of the Rock-aways, Shaindy reflexively locked her door as soon as she saw the panhandlers, junkies, and lanky youth of various ethnicities bopping up and down the streets and sprawling across the stoops. From the windows of the tenement housing rained chicken claws, watermelon rinds and soiled diapers — what the locals dubbed, "air mail."

Fortunately, Shaindy found a parking spot right in front of the pharmacy, and she hoped that this was a harbinger of an expeditious escape from the War Zone. Alas, it was not to be.

At this juncture, a word is in order about parking aptitude, which, compared with her many other talents, was not Shaindy's strong suit. Her parking, like her driving, was heavily influenced by the other players on the field. In other words, her success depended upon everyone else, pedestrians and drivers alike, executing their roles to perfection.

This slight liability, coupled by nervousness about getting into and out of the 'hood sound in mind and body, compounded by the dismally *imperfect* parking on either side of her parking space did not work in her favor. Predictably, Shaindy's tenuous parking career hit a low — indeed "hit" is the operative word — when she heard the sickening sound of metal clangorously impacting upon glass and chrome.

Factually, aside from the left-front headlight, o.b.m., of the vehicle behind her, the damage was not major. But facts were not the natives' primary concern. From the spontaneous, unsolicited reinforcements of the militant-looking troops, one would imagine that a genocidal incursion had just been launched and these brave defenders were going to protect their sacred homeland. Even the drugged-out and the alcoholically sedated were roused from their stupor to exact vengeance from the trespasser.

Justice had finally been afforded to the looting-deprived ghetto inhabitants of the Rockaways. Well, not total justice; they had a shopping list from here to China and were only tossed this token, sacrificial lamb. Life wasn't always fair, *nebbach*.

Reflexively, Shaindy got out to inspect the damage, an instinct not fully governed by self-preservation. In a flash, she felt as if she had been caught in a pyrophobic crowd fleeing toward an exit — which just goes to show that one man's tragedy is another man's tourist attraction.

But that is where the analogy ends, for there was nothing touristy about the mob that was forming and metastasizing. There was a powerful, last-chopper-out-of-Saigon feel to the scene and the sensation was deteriorating to a Newark Riots ambience. Shaindy was definitely on hostile turf and as far as she could see, there was no knight in shining armor — or even in corrosive, low-quality, imported, second-grade, oxidized tin — about to rescue this damsel in mega-distress.

The owner of the damaged vehicle stepped forward accompanied by a solid wall of tattooed biceps. "Yous broke my caaar!" he seethed. Those in the closest vicinity nodded their heads, but it wasn't clear if they were corroborating the assertion, attesting to the fact that the car was actually his or were bobbing to the beat emanating from one of the ubiquitous ghetto-blasters.

"I'm s-s-s-so sorry," Shaindy wanted to say, but her vocal chords were in trachea-arrest. She wished that her car, with her aboard, would morph into a Looney Tunes mobile that would bend going around curves, stretch on takeoff, snap back to normal upon stopping, and defy the laws of physics, gravity and whatever else it would take to get out of the 'hood. Pronto.

BACK from her fantasy and into the grim world of reality, Shaindy reached into her purse to pull out some money, which she fortunately had with her. Best-case scenario, the funds would amply cover the repair, save the hassle of dealing with the insurance company and make amends for the inconvenience. In a flash she realized that quadruple what she had could not placate the looting-deprived mob. They were drawing menacingly closer and in the glow of the street lamp, she could see ice picks and chains materializing.

Upon her return from seminary in Israel, Shaindy had been tempted to register for a Negotiations 101 course in college, but now, in her hour of need, she suspected that it would have had little practical application. She looked yonder one more time, vainly hoping to spot someone from the cavalry who could rescue her. She saw quite the opposite and began to mourn her own demise.

Just then, a nanosecond before it was all over, a voice piped up from the crowd, exclaiming, "Yo man, she's cool. She's cool, I'z tellin' ya' she's cool. Jus' take da money and let da sista go."

Shaindy couldn't see who her rescuer was, but then again, the crowd seemed to blur together before her eyes. But whoever the fellow was, he stood his ground adamantly and the tension subsided. The owner of the damaged car stepped forward and defiantly snatched the cash as if he were settling for a minnow when he could have had a whale. Slowly and raucously, the crowd dispersed and Shaindy resumed breathing.

And there, before her eyes, was her savior — none other than Leroy, the short, stocky hard-working janitor from the West Lawrence Care Center. Leroy, whom Shaindy punctiliously made sure to thank each time she visited for his meticulousness in keeping the building and grounds so neat and clean.

As the proverb goes, "Good words are worth much and cost little." If you would ask Shaindy Berkowitz, she would argue that the adage is an understatement. She is living proof.

Heard from: Esther Lerner

Divine Partnership

COLOR ME astounded as to why the Zaks family — only known descendants of the Chofetz Chaim — gave away what could arguably be considered the Chofetz Chaim's most valuable heirloom. Everyone knows that the Zakses guard their illustrious precursor's sparse possessions zealously and have never permitted memorabilia to leave the family. As a matter of fact, when someone offered half a million dollars for the Chofetz Chaim's *gartel,* the money was flatly and unequivocally refused.

That is why mementos from the Chofetz Chaim are never traded on the market — any market — and cannot be found at auctions, among Judaica dealers, on eBay, or any place else!

Mr. Bernard Dov "Benno" Hochstein, the object's recipient, was a philanthropist supportive of untold worthy causes, a tireless activist on behalf of Israel and perhaps one of *tzedakah*'s greatest ambassadors, but if there was one thing he was definitely *not*, it was a member of the Chofetz Chaim's family.

But Rabbi Yisrael Meir Zaks begged to differ. As the stunned audience sat spellbound at the Chofetz Chaim Yeshivah's annual dinner, Rabbi Zaks declared that the family's time-honored policy was not being violated by presenting Reb Dov with the *Toras Kohanim*. It was the only extant copy from the first printing, a copy signed by the Chofetz Chaim himself and with a warm personal blessing in the frontispiece. Mr. Bernard Hochstein's extraordinary work on behalf of the yeshivah qualified him for all the rights and privileges of a full-fledged family member.

Hochstein, for his part, was deeply moved by the unprecedented gesture. For the rest of his life, the unique gift was a most prized possession.

BERNARD HOCHSTEIN had always been involved in the yeshivah's dinner, although his efforts were never so richly rewarded. With never a thought for recognition nor compensation, he invested tremendous effort and time to ensure that all Chofetz Chaim events would be memorable, successful, and produce maximum return for the yeshivah.

Hochstein's meticulous attention to detail was legend, and if the dinner always ran as smoothly as a finely tuned Formula I racer, it was Bernard Hochstein who was responsible. One year, in his concern for precision, he insisted that Judy, the yeshivah's young secretary, be physically present at the dinner. Her involvement with the reservations and logistics rendered her an indispensable fount of information, and paying the caterer for one extra setting was a small price for all that she would bring to the evening.

Within the opening minutes of the dinner, Hochstein's insistence on Judy's participation had been vindicated, and was further corroborated throughout the night. Judy was invaluable at smoothing out problems that arose, and her knowledge of who had requested to sit with whom, and the pledges that people had made, was crucial information at the most critical time.

Accordingly, Judy was the busiest person at the dinner and got her chance to sit down and eat only toward the end of the main course. Actually, even then "sit down and eat" was wishful thinking, for somewhere between her first and second bites she was called back to the trenches. She had to consult lists and write down details, coordinate individuals, and secure commitments — and it all had to be done right then and there.

Judy was recently engaged and the new *kallah* had much on her head. In her rush that evening, her dearest possession was removed for *netilas yadayim* — but it was never replaced. The poor girl (which would be an accurate description of her financial as well as her emotional state) was to be forgiven. She was not yet accustomed to wearing a ring, any ring, and certainly not an 18 karat white gold, three-stone, princess-cut engagement ring with two princess side-stones and an eight diamond channel-set on the band.

It was not until later that evening that she realized — with a near heart attack — that her ring was missing. With an audible yelp, she dropped everything and dashed to the powder room where she had removed her ring in order to wash. Alas, the object of her frantic search was not there. Not on the counter and not on the floor, not between the cushions, not in the wastepaper basket and not in the sink.

Judy experienced a condition known as soul-pulverization and looked as though she was mourning her own death. Fighting back her tears, she approached the Rosh Yeshivah and asked him what could be done.

There was but one obvious thing that could be done, but Rabbi Zaks hesitated. Dov Hochstein was the master of ceremonies, and his standard was the same each year: a degree of decorum and a precision of protocol that simply had to be maintained. Announcing a missing diamond engagement ring violated both.

Judy stood there, her eyes narrowed in pain, imploring Rabbi Zaks to make the announcement — as if the very mention of a missing ring would cause it to appear — all the while cognizant that waitresses, cleaning ladies, hotel guests and who-knew-who-else had been going in and out of the powder room all evening. They were in New York City, after all, not Bnei Brak. The harsh reality was, if a ring was missing, it was gone.

In fact, the only thing that the announcement would do was distract everyone's attention from the yeshivah's appeal, which was the culmination of months of focused effort and expense.

The other reality was that, at a time like this, it was best not to tangle with Mr. Hochstein who was so instrumental in keeping the yeshivah afloat both personally and as a pillar of the yeshivah dinner's success. Reb Dov was *most* particular regarding how the dinner should run, having the yeshivah's agenda strictly in mind. His philosophy could be boiled down to: the most crucial element in the yeshivah's continued financial stability was next year's dinner, and the greatest factor in the success of next year's dinner was the success of *this* year's dinner.

Accordingly, the affair must be memorable and enjoyable, in good taste — and as smooth and as brief as possible. Addresses, pronouncements, and even greetings that were not absolutely essential and directly connected to the dinner were *verboten*.

RABBI ZAKS' finely honed Talmudic mind was debating all these factors and causing him to vacillate. For poor Judy, of course, the yeshivah, the dinner, and Bernard Hochstein had suddenly faded into the deep background. Her world had just caved in, and she desperately wanted something to be done.

With the greatest timidity, the Rosh Yeshivah approached Mr. Hochstein and explained what had happened. Without a second's hesitation, the dinner chairman made the announcement. Spontaneously, everyone began looking all around their chairs — a response roughly as effective as searching the TriBorough Bridge — but that is what people do when they hear that a ring was lost. The successful dinner concluded with a pall hanging over it because of the secretary's loss.

Fortunately for all, "pall" and "loss" were not part of Bernard Hochstein's repertoire. He was a man of action and he had a pragmatic sense for rectifying problematic situations both minor and major.

This sense was guided by a sublime principle that Mr. Hochstein always applied when confronted with the possibility of a mitzvah.

It could be best summarized as "sharing", although the word doesn't quite convey the idealistic concept that he so firmly believed in and would go to any length to fulfill. Bernard Hochstein believed that a mitzvah was an opportunity, that charity was a privileged opportunity, and that enabling someone to become independent was a mega-privileged opportunity.

Moreover, he maintained, it was both inappropriate and uncouth to keep opportunities of such magnitude to oneself.

Even though it is often easier and more expeditious to simply take care of matters yourself, if the issue was a mitzvah, Reb Dov would always seek outside involvement. Charity is not to be the domain of the selfish. Hochstein was practical and fanatically pragmatic, but even more than pragmatic, he was *ideological.*

A classic test of Bernard's principle came some years later, after the Hochsteins had made aliyah. The husband of their cleaning lady, a professional photographer, was shooting an outdoor wedding at a hotel when one of the inebriated attendees pushed him into the swimming pool. Together with the photographer, the cameras, meters, flash umbrellas, lenses, filters, tripod, and accessories plunged into the water. In one great splash his career was destroyed and his livelihood lost.

The man, just like his cleaning-lady-wife, worked hard to make ends meet. And now, like their photographic equipment, they were ruined. Naturally, the cleaning lady approached Mr. Hochstein for assistance.

As usual, Bernard saw this as an opportunity. Not only was this a chance to help someone, it was an opportunity to put someone back on their feet. It was the proverbial, "Teach a man to fish..."

But according to Hochsteinian dogma, this opportunity had to be shared, and he had just the partner in mind although he had never met the man or even known what he looked like.

IN NEW YORK CITY, as anyone who has listened to radio advertisements in the metropolitan area can attest, there is a photography equipment superstore. Closed from Friday afternoon through Saturday, this world-renowned establishment was obviously owned by a Sabbath observing Jew. *He* would be the ideal partner to share in this rare and precious undertaking.

Hochstein called the store, which comprises a full block of prime Manhattan real estate, and asked to speak to the owner —

an act somewhat akin to calling the White House and asking to speak to the tenant.

Only thanks to Hochstein's incredible persistence did he eventually, actually, prevail. This would not be a long conversation, the New York tycoon made very clear. Hochstein sketched the situation very quickly and lay at the proprietor's feet an uncommon opportunity to help a deserving Jew in *Eretz Yisrael*. But the superstore owner, who had never heard of Bernard Hochstein and was unfamiliar with his reputation, deemed the tale "fishy" — an unfortunate term to describe five-digits-worth of waterlogged photographic equipment.

With a healthy skepticism regarding the story's veracity, the camera king of Manhattan did not see himself as a candidate for Hochstein's glorious opportunity. He had a benign formula for nudniks which he recited to the unknown caller at the other end of the line, "I can't give from my business, but come to my door during the charity hours and I hope I can be of some help."

Before the click of finality, Hochstein

asserted, "My dear sir, are you not from Satmar, a community that cherishes the mitzvah of *tzedakah*? It behooves you to help this needy individual. I could easily fund this by myself, but as Providence has placed you in *this* line of work, I seek you as my partner in the mitzvah."

It was a bold appeal, heavy on the temerity, but the photography-enterprise-entrepreneur remained unconvinced. The man was also pressed for time as he was in the midst of investigating a more routine partnership opportunity. He therefore declined this one with a curt "Goodbye."

Reb Dov, for his part, was becoming quite indignant. He sought a partner and had found what he deemed to be the perfect candidate, but the nominee refused to serve. Uncharacteristically, Bernard might have even been willing to entertain the notion of a nominal partnership, but he never got the chance.

THE HOCHSTEIN CHILDREN tried to calm their father down, but to no avail. They knew that they had as much chance of persuading him to drop the mitzvah as they had of persuading the Mormon Tabernacle Choir to dedicate a number to *Yad L'Achim*. But the "partnership" ideal was only viable if the other partner was willing to tango, and Mr. Superstore was not even willing to set foot on the dance floor.

The kids begged their father to be more realistic and concede, but he would not capitulate. Capitulate, shmapitulate, the reader (that's you) may be thinking: you can lead a horse to water... but a stranger cannot force a stranger to give money to a stranger.

Generally that would be a safe assessment — *except* when it came to Bernard Hochstein.

It was never — to borrow from basketball jargon — an even match up. The photo exec had to cope with accounts payable and receivable, inventory, advertising, salespeople, salary, utility expenses, rent, catalogue production, Web-expansion, training, floor displays, and a host of other business-related matters while Bernard Hochstein had only to deal with the plight of his cleaning lady's husband. He was totally absorbed with the matter and nothing else at the time was of importance to him.

Since Hochstein was never one to bar any sort of hold when it came to *mitzvos*, he pulled out all the stops and uncharacteristically called Rabbi Zaks in New York. As a rule, Bernard never liked to trouble the Chofetz Chaim Rosh Yeshivah, or anyone for that matter, but a mitzvah opportunity was at stake.

"Do you have any connections with the owner of that large photo store in Manhattan?" Reb Dov wanted to know. Rabbi Zaks didn't, but he wasn't going to let Bernard know that. The way, the only way, to ever pay Mr. Hochstein back was by enabling him to perform a mitzvah and right now — within the rabbi's clutches — was payday!

The Rosh Yeshivah was ready to turn the world upside down, and he nearly did, one connection leading to another connection until he reached the connection that had the key to the door.

Rabbi Zaks was able to explain to the

store owner not only precisely who it was that had called him so many times from Jerusalem, but also that he was up against an unstoppable force who — fortunately — was always working for the good guys. After this background, a story that had previously sounded fishy was now fully-filleted, and the executive wanted nothing more than to jump enthusiastically into the kettle.

"I'll provide the equipment at cost price," Mr. Superstore said to Rabbi Zaks, "which I will be delighted to split with Mr. Hochstein 50–50."

Without even so much as a sigh, Bernard moved on to the next step. There was now a rather large load of heavy, bulky, and expensive equipment that had to be transported to Israel. It filled several suitcases and would be subject to heavy duties at customs.

Reb Dov requested Rabbi Zaks to continue the partnership for this stage of the operation and he prodded him to arrange an expeditious delivery. For the Rosh Yeshivah the opportunity was golden and he deftly negotiated the transport.

There was nothing that could have pleased Bernard more. Hochstein spoke about gratitude often and he certainly practiced what he preached.

It was as if Rabbi Zaks, whose yeshivah was able to function thanks to the largesse and devotion of Bernard Hochstein, had done the philanthropist the greatest and most vital favor in the world. People whose lives were saved didn't thank their benefactors as much as Hochstein thanked the Rosh Yeshivah. He must have thanked him a hundred times, maybe more.

AND SO, the very same Bernard Dov Hochstein who knew how to curtail the grief of the yeshivah secretary with the writing of one check, would not do so if it conflicted with his modus operandi. As always, he sought *a partner.*

At the yeshivah dinner was one of Mr. Hochstein's most notable comrades in alms, Mr. Yankel Melohn. The two of them were closely aligned with the yeshivah and many other *chessed* and *tzedakah* projects, most notably the construction of *mikvaos*.

After consulting for a few seconds at most, they decided that they would jointly cover the cost of the engagement ring, to the tune of $3,600, and both were delighted at the opportunity.

They would not need any letters or uncomfortable phone calls reminding them of their "pledge." Right then and there they settled the matter so that Judy could go out and buy a new ring with her groom none the wiser.

THE NEXT DAY Rabbi Zaks received a phone call.

"Hello."

"Hello, Rabbi Zaks?"

"Speaking."

"Rabbi Zaks, this is H. M."

"Hello, Mrs. M. How are you?"

"I'm fine, Rabbi Zaks."

"Good. Good. How can I help you, Mrs. M.?"

"Well you know, Rabbi, I was at the yeshivah dinner last night..."

"Yes, I recall seeing you briefly."

"Yes, of course. Well, anyway, Rabbi, an odd thing happened to me last night."

"Really?"

"It was in the, uh, ladies room. Well, the sink outside the ladies room, that is."

"And?"

"Well you see, I found a ring, a diamond..."

With that, the Rosh Yeshivah smacked his forehead so hard, that Mrs. M. heard the echo through the phone. "You found a what!?" he managed to whisper.

"A diamond ring. An engagement ring,

I'd say, and from the look of it, a very *expensive* one. Now, I don't really know diamonds, Rabbi, but..."

"My dear Mrs. M., didn't you hear the announcement?"

"What announcement?"

"We announced that a diamond engagement ring had gone missing and asked that if anyone had found it, they bring it to Mr. Hochstein."

"Oh... well, I left early, Rabbi. I guess I didn't hear the announcement."

"And the ring?"

"I knew it belonged to *someone*, Rabbi. I mean, diamond rings don't just grow on trees, now, do they?"

With every word spoken by the well-intentioned Mrs. M., Rabbi Zaks' exasperation increased exponentially. Where was the ring, he wanted to know.

"And so you..."

"What?"

"And so you..."

"And so I what?"

"And so you did *what* with the ring?"

"And so I dropped the ring into my purse
— for safekeeping."

"Where is the ring now!?" he wanted to
shout as he bit his lower lip.

"I was afraid that someone might steal
it, so I dropped it into my purse for safekeeping. We had to leave early, you see. My
daughter-in-law's brother..."

"Mrs. M.?" very quietly, with maximum
control.

"Yes, Rabbi?"

"Where is the ring now?"

"Why it's in Saul's safe, Rabbi, down at
the office."

"I see. It's in Mr. M.'s safe. And why didn't you report having found it?"

"That's exactly what I'm doing, Rabbi. You see, I had my aerobics class this morning, low-impact, of course, and the aerobics is right next to the supermarket, so I *always* do my weekly grocery..."

"I see," sighing.

"And now I'm home, and I called to report finding the ring, first thing..."

"Thank you, Mrs. M. Thank you *very* much."

BECAUSE Rabbi Zaks had nothing quite as pressing as aerobics, shopping and daughter-in-law's brother's neighbor's whatever, he was not about to delay — for even a second — and made three consecutive phone calls. The young secretary nearly fainted when she heard that she would be getting her *real* ring back and not be causing any expense to Messrs. Hochstein and Melohn.

The Rosh Yeshivah next telephoned Mr.

Hochstein — a very rare call indeed. How often did Yisrael Meir Zaks get to offer Dov Hochstein eighteen hundred dollars? The Rosh Yeshivah reached the philanthropist and informed him that the ring was found and that, of course, the check would not be cashed.

Reb Dov's response was not as expected. "What exactly will Judy's husband be doing once they are married?" he wanted to know.

"He will be learning in *kollel*."

"If that's the case," Reb Dov said with the lilt of joy that Rabbi Zaks knew so well, "then her hours of anxiety will be rewarded with a few extra dollars to enable her husband's learning."

Rabbi Zaks then called Mr. Melohn with the good and ironic news that *he* was offering him money. Melohn wanted to know what Hochstein was doing with his half. When he heard the classic Hoschsteinian response, Mr. Melohn decided to continue the partnership.

Essentially, that was the life of Bernard Hochstein: forming partnerships and sharing for the benefit of others.

His very first partnership, the one that molded all subsequent ones, occurred when he was a bar mitzvah boy.

ALL BY HIMSELF, as nervous and excited thirteen-year-old Benno entered a shul in Amsterdam in order to put on *tefillin* for the very first time. His father attended the synagogue only on Shabbos, and made no exception on that occasion.

The milestone did not go totally unnoticed; as an elderly *talmid chacham* approached Benno to extend a mazel tov. After initial pleasantries, the scholar inquired if the young boy understood the prayers he was reciting.

Benno hadn't a clue, but that was about to change. Yisroel Aronson, childless and a widower from a young age, invited the youngster to learn Torah with him. Rabbi Aronson embodied the values of the

Slabodka Yeshivah where he had studied and never exchanged them for the norms of the corporate workplace where he made his living.

He would work in the beginning of the week (a little) at the diamond exchange. Once he had earned enough to sustain himself for that week he would retire from mundane pursuits and dedicate the rest of the week to Torah study. Even the few days a week that he *did* work, were primarily devoted to learning.

For fourteen years, Benno studied at the feet of Rabbi Aronson in the rabbi's extremely modest apartment every evening. Aronson, for his part, would not hear of accepting any compensation for his caring tutelage. For nearly a decade and a half, Benno absorbed Torah learning, values, and priorities from a master teacher and became Yisroel Aronson's spiritual heir.

THE NEXT PARTNERSHIP would occur in 1938, when Benno visited the United States. He was already a young man in his twenties exploring possibilities for emigrating to America to avoid an ominous and looming future in Europe. Bernard called upon a relative in New York City, object: accommodations. The man agreed, but with great reluctance.

The host was quick to clarify that he would be away for the weekend in Atlantic Beach, and that the lodging would not be available *in absentia*. Benno offered to come along and, although the bid was not rejected out of hand, the terms were not negotiable: Dov could come only if he would pay for himself.

Spending a weekend in an Atlantic Beach hotel might just teach him more about America, Bernard reasoned, in his attempt to justify the expense. He had no idea how right he was.

When he arrived at the hotel, Hochstein met a young bachelor and inquired if he would mind sharing a room with him in order to economize. The fellow, although Benno could not have known it at the time, had the family resources to purchase the hotel, but Moe Feuerstein still agreed.

Feuerstein's behavior in general, and one

specific act in particular, would profoundly shape the destiny of Bernard Hochstein.
On Shabbos morning, prior to the reading
of the Torah, Moe Feuerstein, in an act typical of a life that would be dedicated to the
Jewish People, delivered an appeal for the
Chevron yeshivah.

Hochstein was gape-jawed by this
young, single man — younger than he
— shamelessly arising before an audience
of adults and pressing them to contribute
generously to a cause they had never even
heard of before. Then and there Hochstein
resolved that he too would like to be dynamically involved in worthwhile causes.

Bernard returned to Europe, but managed to escape with his wife to the West
shortly before it was too late. They were tumultuous times, but Bernard never forgot
what he witnessed and the pledge that he
had made to himself.

ON FRIDAY, September 5, 2008, Bernard
Hochstein was summoned to the Great
Partner for Whom he had worked all his
life. Large segments of the Jewish People
came to pay their respects. Rabbi Zaks flew

to Israel for the sole purpose of honoring his friend and benefactor and comforting the members of the Hochstein family. During the *shiva* he inquired if the *brachah* from the Chofetz Chaim was still in the house. "Of course," Dov's children replied with pride, and removed the Chofetz Chaim's personalized *sefer* from the shelf.

One of the assembled cautioned that they should be very careful to not let the book out of sight as there is always a tumult in a *beis avel* and things can disappear. At the time it sounded like a rather alarmist warning.

On a Thursday morning, the Hochstein family arose from *shiva* and departed to the Mount of Olives to their father's gravesite for the traditional *azkarah* service. As Rabbi Zaks delivered a eulogy, his words were interrupted by the ring of a cell phone. The minor interruption evolved into major disruption as the family began to huddle.

With admirable self-control, Rabbi Yisroel Meir Zaks continued his farewell as the impromptu symposium eventually dispersed. How could the Rosh Yeshivah have known that the family was doing everything it could to prevent him from learning what the hullabaloo was all about?

THE NIGHT BEFORE, the celebrated *Toras Kohanim* had disappeared from the *shiva* house. No one said a word to Rabbi Zaks to spare him anguish, but there was angst aplenty among the Hochsteins. It was a painful denouement to a calamitous week.

At first they thought that the *sefer* was simply misplaced. Only after extensive searches were they able to determine that the book was, in fact, missing. At that point, the family began to marshal their connections to locate the *sefer*.

They were aided by the fact that one of the grandchildren had taken random photographs of those who attended the *beis avel*. The pictures were being carefully scrutinized, particularly in light of the fact that a different grandchild reported that one of the assembled asked numerous questions about the *sefer* and from the time of his inquiries the book was unaccounted for.

A different grandchild did her share by

calling in an old favor. A senior psychologist in the Israeli Ministry of Health, she was once asked to visit a woman imprisoned for tax-evasion who was not faring well. The oppressive environment — the constant humiliation from the guards, and cellmates from the very dregs of society — were driving the imprisoned woman into deep depression.

In her position, Shifra was entitled to visit when she pleased and was not limited by the strictures of prison visitation regulations. The convict, who worked with her husband in the Judaica manuscripts business, claimed that Shifra's visit saved her sanity. When she was released from prison, she attempted to repay Shifra for her kindness, but the psychologist staunchly refused.

On the last night of Reb Dov's *shiva*, Shifra accessed her connection to rare Judaica literature. She requested from her one-time acquaintance to get the word out that the precious *Toras Kohanim* was at large.

THE NEXT MORNING, as the family convened at the cemetery, the dealer that

Shifra had assisted received a phone call from one of her colleagues. The caller reported that a man was at his house, offering to sell him a first edition copy of *Toras Kohanim*. Although the book was unequivocally genuine, it did not have the stamp of the Radin Yeshiva as the one stolen from the Hochsteins reportedly did.

Shifra's Judaica connection was not deterred by the discrepancy. A thief, she reasoned, would probably tear out the page with the stamp to disguise the book's origin. The dealer did not need to hear another word. "You have fifteen minutes," he uttered sternly to the would be vendor, "to return the book to its rightful owners. They know who you are and they have your picture; if the book is not in their hands within a quarter of an hour you will be arrested."

The thief claimed that he was far too embarrassed to return the *sefer*. "Then find an alternate way to get it back," the dealer warned. "The deadline of fifteen minutes remains. After that you will have to explain yourself to the police."

Within the prescribed time period, the

brachah of the Chofetz Chaim was safely back home. It returned to the family of a man who was *truly* blessed and who wished — indeed, insisted — upon making everyone his partner so that he could share his blessing.

Heard from: Rabbi Yisrael Meir Zaks and BenZion Hochstein

Awesome

Stanley Kup

FOR MANY KIDS, as spring slouches into summer the mental fan belt comes loose, leading before long to all sorts of other cerebral trouble. The brain, on overload with the mounting ruminations of camp, has no more sockets left for the schoolwork switch. Simply put, teachers of math and social studies cannot compete with the scent of leather and bubble gum and images of a ball arcing gracefully through the air and sliding perfectly through the rim, rippling the bottom of the net with a distinctive, thrilling swish.

Camp Monroe* is one such end-of-the-year school-buster, causing hundreds of students to slide into a state of mental atrophy as they anticipate departing for their favorite place on earth. It has a rich history in this regard, as it has been catering to Jewish youngsters for over six decades as one of the original kosher camps in America. Over the years the clientele became less observant, perhaps because of the proliferation of other, non-coed camps that attracted campers from more religious homes. But in 1982, when the majority of the camp's owners became *ba'alei teshuvah* (newly religious), Camp Monroe underwent a subtle metamorphosis. It was no longer kosher-style but *glatt* kosher; Saturday turned into Shabbos.

Today, a religious visitor to the camp would be hard-pressed to find pronounced expressions of religiosity, but considering the hyper-assimilated background of the campers and the lifestyle of their parents, the subtle strides the camp makes to present genuine observance in a positive, non-

---

* Actual name. All names used in this story are genuine.

threatening way are really not so subtle.

This does not happen gratis. Whatever the necessary profit margin is for a camp to be financially viable, Camp Monroe swallows a loss for what it considers a critical gain: inspiring youngsters in their Jewish heritage. The results of this policy are modest and diverse. Here is one.

'TWAS THE VERY stately Lord Stanley of Preston, otherwise known as the Sixteenth Earl of Derby, Queen Victoria's appointment of Governor General of Canada, who originally proposed the idea of a champion cup for the top hockey team in Canada. This evolved into the highest honor awarded in professional hockey, known as the "Stanley Cup." About a hundred years after Lord Stanley's proposal, Stanley Felsinger the First, director and head counselor of Camp Monroe in Orange County, New York, proposed the creation of the "Stanley Kup" for the winner of the inter-camp street-hockey tournament. And like the annual Boat Race between Oxford and Cambridge, the Army–Navy football rivalry and the Duke vs. North Carolina basketball competition, the Stanley Kup became the sporting highlight of the (camp) season.

Stanley Kup in Yiddish means "Stanley's head," but the wit of the pun has been lost over the years and the championship has been anglicized to the conventional "Stanley Cup." For a period of two full months, the teams practice on a daily basis, sometimes twice a day, in preparation for the tournament.

All the preparation and all of the practice, all of the dedication and all of the perseverance come down to one final championship game played before the entire camp. Pressure? You bet. Prestige? In spades. Cliffhanger? Usually not.

As the host, Camp Monroe not only has the home-team advantage, but always boasts the honed-team advantage; in other words, a cohesive group of players who work together like a well-oiled machine, and who are reared on an amalgam of the good sportsmanship that the camp promotes and the sporting excellence that the tournament demands.

In 1991, however, Monroe had neither

an advantage nor a chance. Their oppo-
nent, Camp Kinder Ring, won all of their
preliminary games with ease and were the
undisputed favorite for the Stanley Cup.
Still, for tradition's sake, Camp Monroe
would put up their best fight and every single camper would be rooting for them.

At supper prior to the game, the meal —
as in, the food served — was purely inciden-
tal. A pep rally was conducted that would
have been the envy of any high school in
a state championship. Boisterous chants
thundered through the dining hall as if it
were outfitted with speakers of Woodstock
caliber. Bunk after bunk climbed upon
their benches and mimicked the classic
cheer motions of Lunge, High V, Left Di-
agonal, Right Punch and Touchdown. No
efforts were made to curb the campers' enthusiasm. Sheer pandemonium reigned.

The spirit was indescribable, and every
camper was already hoarse from shouting
the chants and shrieking the camp song at
the top of their lungs. And yet... everyone
knew that Monroe was the distinct underdog. It would take a miracle just to lose by a
non-embarrassing differential.

STANLEY FELSINGER was thinking the same thing, but from a different perspective. Since a miracle was definitely called for, he was wondering what could be done to earn that extra measure of Providence. Some head counselors worry about how to get their campers spirited; Stanley worried about his campers' spirits. Not for naught was the series named after his head.

And it was precisely that head that was strategizing how to earn a miracle. The idea that he devised was, well, unconventional. He turned to the coach, Neil Levinbook, and requested that the team attend the *Minchah* services prior to the game.

"But that means they'll be late for the warm-ups," the coach was about to protest, until he saw the look on Stanley's face. He then understood that the proposal was an instruction, and *not* a suggestion.

Truth be told, the hockey team was not composed of the most devout campers in Camp Monroe, and the majority of them had participated in a *Minchah* service about as often as they had recited *Birkas Hachamah*. For boys who had become bar mitzvah without even contemplating God, the proposal of *Minchah* on this evening was viewed much the way Captain Ahab thought of Moby Dick.

Still, Stanley, the man who generally had a special finesse about not foisting religion, persisted. With no other recourse the team, with about as much enthusiasm as an emphysemic displays for cigar smoke, lumbered into the small room affectionately known as "the shul." The coach and his assistant, plus fifteen players outfitted in full hockey gear, awkwardly placed shiny, pointed *kippo*s on their heads and took the prayer books they were handed. It was all beginning to feel like a polite hijacking.

Coach Levinbook was still feeling that the sudden burst of religious fervor — well, to be honest, the expression on the players' faces was far more akin to a heart patient doped up for a bypass — was a strategic mistake. Extracting fifteen psyched players from the frenzy of the pep rally to the quiet seclusion of a prayer service would be like sucking the air and buoyancy out of a zeppelin. But Stanley the First never had a *quiet* service in mind.

A sportsman himself and former starter for Columbia's varsity basketball team, he was fully cognizant of the rule that "half of the battle is won before you get onto the court." Stanley definitely had something up his sleeve.

"Gentlemen," he began, "this evening we have a lot to pray for. The fact is that we always have a lot to pray for, but now we have a special opportunity to acquire a perspective that would otherwise pass us by. When you want to win and you are the underdog, your only hope is to play better and harder than you ever have, with no room for error.

"But how can a player exceed his abilities?" Stanley slowly looked around the room as if he were about to reveal a deep, dark secret. He was.

"A person is bound by *their* limitations unless they can break free and become *someone else*. All of us have the ability to become a better, and hence a *different* person, breaking the shackles of our past. The old Camp Monroe could not beat Kinder Ring, but in the few remaining minutes before the game, we can commence the process of transformation that will free us from our earlier constrictions."

There were a few expressions of "Huh?" but by and large the team caught his drift.

"When I say 'different,'" he continued, his voice increasing an octave, "I really mean 'better.' One who improves his behavior and character is more deserving of Divine favor than one who does not. Thus, if we go into this prayer service committing ourselves to enhance our moral sensitivity, adhere to a code of ethics and increase our spiritual observance, we will become greater individuals — indeed, different people than we were before, and more deserving of our prayers being answered."

Stanley's eyes burn brightest when he talks about religious concepts, and now the wattage became contagious. All across the room looks of boredom were replaced with intense concentration. If you could ignore the padding, hockey sticks and jerseys, the Camp Monroe shul suddenly took on the ambience of a *shtiebel* on Yom Kippur. The spiritual firepower in that room could have illuminated a *beis midrash*.

When *Minchah* was concluded, the team was even more energized than they had been emerging from the pep rally. Stanley wasn't about to lose this moment; he immediately suggested that the team remain to pray the *Maariv* service.

It was two minutes to face-off, and by rights the butterflies in their stomachs should have already been fluttering. But the team, as a man, decided to stay put and offer yet additional devotions, rendering this the most prayer-intensive day of (most of) their lives.

BACK IN THE fan-frenzied arena no one knew what had happened to the team. Kinder Ring assumed that their opponents were too intimidated to arrive for their humiliation. No one could have fathomed how the CM players were preparing for the match.

When the *Maariv* service was completed the team, humbled but confident, marched out. They were twenty minutes late.

Kinder Ring's hubris was met by Monroe's tenacity. CM played like a well-choreographed, united team, one player always covering for another. Several times the opponents rallied, but they could not penetrate Monroe's defense.

After the first period Kinder Ring's coach must have read his players the riot act and threatened to dock canteen and lake privileges for the rest of the summer. They returned to the rink with blood in their eyes and springs in their legs. Throughout the period they controlled the hockey ball and in the early minutes KR's center managed to wing off a shot before CM's goalie was adequately prepared. *Zing!* The goalie raised his arm to protect himself — and miraculously the hockey ball caromed off his super-sized catch glove.

It was a spectacular save but just seconds later the right wing fired a bullet at the goal, low and to the left. CM's goalie dropped to the ground, his legs splayed out in a split. He recoiled from the pain, but his left leg pad had smothered the hockey ball. Even with his padded hockey pants, shoulder pads, shin guards, elbow pads, wrist guards, helmet and hockey gloves, the goalkeeper was taking a pounding.

Monroe was unable to rally a significant offense as Kinder Ring created more and more scoring opportunities. They were slipping shots between their legs and intimidating the Monroe goalkeeper. One KR player uncorked a cannon toward his teammate, who received the pass deep into Monroe territory. He ran three steps closer to the goal and at nearly point blank range wound up in full flight, and fired. Monroe's goalie instinctively flashed his glove out and grabbed it. It was a phenomenal save but it was past the goal mouth, representing a score for Kinder Ring.

The Monroe players had done an enviable job of reigning in Kinder Ring and keeping the score even, but now that the opponents had grabbed the lead the camp rallied to their team's aid. On defense they chanted, "T-A-K-E, Take that ball away." On offense they alternated between, "1-2-3-4 Shoot the ball, Come on, Let's Score!" and "Pass, run, shoot to score, Make a goal, We want more!"

The second period ended with Kinder Ring still ahead with a menacing one-point lead. The third and final period began with impossible pressure on Monroe; Kinder Ring had morphed from formidable opponents to monsters. As all of Monroe's attempts at scoring had been foiled early on, they decided to go for broke with a risky maneuver. "We're going to do a player change on the fly," the center repeated the coach's instructions. "The third time that we get possession in our zone, you get the hockey ball to me," he said to the right wing, "and head for the bench. When he gets within ten feet, Brian, you hop out onto the rink, and I'll feed you the hockey ball for a clean breakaway."

Playing decoy, the Monroe left wing lost the hockey ball on purpose. As planned, KR got excited at their sudden scoring chance, sending one of their defenders into the forward zone. The Monroe right wing managed to steal the hockey ball from him when KR made a drop pass. He then fed the center and headed for the sideline. Nobody followed him, for all the KR players were focusing on the center.

"Go for it!" the center hissed as Brian jumped onto the rink. At that precise moment the center fed him the hockey ball — a long, perfect pass — and Brian grabbed it.

Only one defender stood between him and the goal. Instead of trying to fake him out — which was how Brian kept losing the hockey ball in the first two periods — he tried to outrace him.

Brian went around the player's right side and the huge, unwieldy defenseman could not keep up. Brian could hear all of the KR players yelling, and it sounded like music to his ears. He focused like a laser on the spot he wanted to shoot for and then let the ball fly.

Bull's-eye! Score! Tie game!

In a flash Brian was mobbed by his teammates and one half of the audience broke into the camp theme song. Tying the game brought about an unexpected disadvantage to Kinder Ring, who began to play recklessly in their attempt to score that one final goal that would earn them the Stanley

Cup. Each of KR's scoring stars tried to win the game all by themselves, while Monroe stayed together as a team.

WHEN THERE was only one minute left to the game KR finally launched a full-team attack. It wasn't an especially prudent move, but with fifty-four seconds left, KR tossed prudence to the wind. KR found its opportunity and let a shot fly. The CM goalie just managed to make the save.

The hockey ball slid out past Monroe's left wing and center, past Kinder Ring — all the way to Brian, and the kid felt his heart leap into his throat. He took off, for no one was back on defense!

A KR player raced out from the other side of the rink to try and cut Brian off before he could launch a shot. Just as he approached, Brian fed the hockey ball a little ahead of himself, then did a full 360-degree spin as if he was on ice.

The move surprised the KR player so much that he tripped and fell to the court at Brian's feet! Brian leapt over the prone body, grabbed the hockey ball and let loose a stinging shot. The KR goalie tried in vain to get a glove on it, but the hockey ball was speeding too fast. The ball hit the back of the net — score! Seconds later the ref blew his whistle three times. Time was up and the championship was over!

Simply put, the crowd went insane. Older and younger campers, kids from competing bunks — anyone and everyone went into a crazy dance, hugging and laughing; some were even crying. Remarkably, the hockey team was less euphoric and Brian, Monroe's sole scorer, was not hoisted into the air. Soberly they trotted over to Stanley and Coach Levinbook, where an ocean of silence arose amid the din of victory in the home arena. "What does this mean?" was etched into their furrowed brows.

Before Stanley could say a thing to his beloved campers, the coach, all of twenty-four years old but sounding like an elderly statesman, sonorously pronounced, "The first goal was *Minchah*, the second goal was *Maariv*!" The team then emitted a spontaneous roar.

Ever since that night, it has become a

tradition for Monroe's hockey team to attend both *Minchah* and *Maariv* services
prior to the final game of the Stanley Cup
tournament. And with this tradition goes
a legend: whoever prays to become a better
person will be victorious in life.

Heard from: Stanley Felsinger

Misleading Appearance

A REFLECTION PERHAPS, of New Age agoraphobics, the Kleiner Shtiebel in Bnei Brak was as crowded as a synagogue could be. The Kleiner Shtiebel was named after its benefactor, who definitely must have been clairvoyant. After all, the honorable gentleman, whose last name means small, had the prescience to endow *this* house of worship. However, the scarcity of space did nothing to distract throngs from attending: from the erudite to the unschooled (there are those, too, in Bnei Brak) — and most everyone in between.

Berman and Etzioni, two of the regulars, would never have met had it not been for Kleiner's. Their backgrounds, professions, outlooks and aspirations were completely opposite. Dr. Joel Berman had graduated from one of America's finer medical schools, and retired to Israel at a relatively young age to engage in the holy pursuit of learning Torah. Rami Etzioni, over twenty years Berman's junior, was an ambitious and smooth-talking Israeli-born Judaica merchant.

Etzioni befriended Berman, at first, with a clearly self-serving goal in mind. He wished to consult an American (a species at a premium in Bnei Brak) about several matters germane to his U.S.-based livelihood. He wasn't looking just for procedure; he wanted to know how the American mindset operated. But over the years he had learned to respect Dr. Berman's multifaceted personality and intelligence, and had consulted him on matters other than business.

And so it was that Rami approached his erudite friend about a halachic problem that he would soon encounter. The following week he would be departing to the United States on one of his periodic trips, this one entitled in his mind "The Mother of all Road Trips." According to plan, he would be clocking over 800 miles of driving from Santa Barbara to San Diego, from Burbank to Beverly Hills.

The days would be devoted to cultivating relationships, socializing with former customers and selling merchandise wherever possible. In Rami's line of work, a personal relationship was not just advantageous, it was essential. There was no standard price for antique Judaica, and no baseline to calibrate against.

Objects were bought and sold as a function of faith and confidence in the merchant. How could one really know if a *kiddush* cup from the eighteenth century had an original hammered finish or one that was added later? Who knew if a silver *Yad* (Torah pointer) with inset letters in the Renaissance style was from the fifteenth or the seventeenth century? How do you determine if a *Megillah* from the Island of Rhodes is as unique as purported? If the item is not exactly as represented, the difference in value could easily be upwards of $50,000.

Because it is so critical to trust the Judaica dealer — and sales hinge upon that faith — relationships are as important as the products. If anyone was aware of this it was Rami Etzioni. He was driven to succeed and he learned early on that trust was the only path.

Accordingly, large blocks of his forthcoming trip were allocated to customer relations and he was convinced that the time invested would always pay high financial dividends. For this he was prepared. However, he was unprepared for a potential difficulty that arose with getting there.

HIS OUTBOUND FLIGHT was an early morning departure on *Yom Tov sheini* — in other words, *motza'ei Shavuos* in Eretz Yisrael. And whereas boarding the plane posed no problem to an Israeli like himself, as the holiday had already concluded, landing overseas on what was still the second day of *Shavuos* was a different story. "What should I do?" he asked Dr. Berman.

Joel thought for but a moment or two and replied, "The best solution, indeed the only real solution, is not to fly on *Yom Tov sheini*."

Rami rejected this solution out of hand. "There was a special on this flight, it was a great deal, and I already have been issued a non-refundable ticket."

"Did it ever occur to you why there was a special on this particular flight?!" Dr. Berman was about to say, and then held back. "Listen Rami," he said instead, "we are long-time friends and I am truly interested in your welfare. That is why my first recommendation is that you change your flight. But if you are not willing to do that, then I can at least apprise you of your halachic options."

"Go ahead."

"Technically, you are permitted to board a plane on *Yom Tov sheini* in Israel. You are even allowed to fly and land abroad. But the Rabbis have forbidden the passenger from departing from the Arrivals Terminal, and they must wait there until *Yom Tov* ends at their landing destination. Since you have an early morning flight, it will land in the U.S. around noon. That means you will have to remain at the airport and may not do any *melachah* in public— no speaking on the phone, no using the computer — just sit and learn or sleep on a bench for the next nine hours. If you are prepared to do this, it is a solution."

"No can do," or thereabouts, Etzioni responded. "I connect from Newark to L.A. right away. It's part of the deal. If I don't use that leg I will have to buy an exorbitant one-way ticket to the West Coast."

"I'm not sure," Berman commented matter-of-factly, "indeed I have *no* idea, why you are asking my advice. You have already made up your mind what you plan to do and therefore my input is irrelevant."

Etzioni was taken aback by Dr. Berman's stinging remark and he fumbled, "Well, um... I was hoping you could give me a pointer or two on how best to do things according to what I've already arranged."

"Rami, I'm very sorry, but I am unable to

alleviate your conscience. There are some significant halachic problems involved in what you intend to do, all of which are governed by the prohibition of *makom she-nahagu*. When the Rabbis require that one adopt the laws of where one presently is and not where one comes from, it is not to be taken lightly. The halachic characterization is *afeelu b'chadrei chadorim* — meaning this injunction applies even where no one will see, even enclosed in an interior room. I really wouldn't be flippant about this."

There was an ominous tone to Dr. Berman's advice, and although Rami had grown to respect the middle-aged, reflective American, all his life he had taken a cavalier attitude toward the advice of elders, especially when it flew in the face of his entrepreneurial aspirations.

Berman assumed all along that Rami knew that what he was planning to do was wrong. Perhaps that's why he posed the question to him and not a local rabbi, figuring that an American would be more compromising than a Bnei Brak native.

In any event, when Dr. Berman saw Rami

in shul on *Yom Tov* he wished him well on his forthcoming trip.

THE TRIP the following day ended up being rather hitch-less and uneventful. The international flight arrived on time and the connection in Newark was perfect. By 4:30 in the afternoon on the second day of *Shavuos*, Rami was already checked in to L.A.'s Sofitel on the corner of La Cienega and Beverly Boulevards. Despite his exhaustion, he was enjoying what the hotel had to offer in French accoutrements and Hollywood glamour.

Once *Yom Tov* was over in California he could make a few phone calls to his exclusively religious clientele, but now it was time to recoup from the flights. This involved taking full advantage of the hotel's amenities, and before long Rami was down to his basics and shaving in the bathroom.

But because his shaver was set to European current it caused a rather violent, albeit localized reaction in the outlet, which began spurting smoke. His wits about him, Rami called down to the front desk, for he knew that there were smoke detectors which would trigger men in yellow charging through his door. The concierge referred the call to the on-duty manager, who appreciated the heads-up for she had already noticed an alarm light blinking in Etzioni's room.

And so could he. Within seconds silver lights began to flash and a deafening alarm began ringing in the room; the smoke detector was just outside the bathroom door. After Rami's repeated assurances that everything was fine the manager performed a "reset" and the fire alarm fell silent.

Meanwhile, Rami had to cope with a billow of annoying smoke in his room and, as in many hotels, opening a window was a tricky maneuver. He therefore abandoned his initial plan in favor of letting the smoke out into the hallway. In retrospect, this idea could be labeled "career error." Unlike the room alarm, smoke in a public hallway is picked up by sensors that report directly to the fire department.

It is not standard operating procedure for the LAFD to place a call to verify if a fire alarm might have been accidentally trig-gered from an outlet where a 220 voltage appliance was inserted. Actually, standard procedure is to respond immediately. But in this case, even that standard procedure was not deemed adequately standard.

Just a few months earlier a fire had bro-ken out on an upper story of a Los Angeles hotel, and by the time it was finally brought under control there were two fatalities, fourteen injuries and $23.7 million worth of damage. The way the media reported it, the Fire Department's ineptitude was responsible for turning what should have been an easy-to-contain fire into a major conflagration. TV crews and reporters were already on the scene and reporting before the first hook and ladder arrived.

It had been Embarrassment City for the LAFD and the Fire Chief was the whipping boy for every local and state politician. He struggled tenaciously to hold on to his po-sition, and publicly vowed that this would *never* happen again.

So as Rami stood stymied in the bath-room wondering what he would do with a fritzed shaver, a multi-alarm fire was being frantically reported to all the firehouses in the vicinity of the Beverly Center. Down Rodeo Drive, across Melrose Avenue and up Sunset Boulevard fire engines were scrambling at full throttle. On their heels were the news networks, anxious to get the first scoop on a breaking story.

RAMI WAS AMAZED by the noise pollution and commotion that plagued the streets of L.A. Every civilized pocket of the world has sirens, but never of this amplitude and number. It was absolutely outrageous! And whereas sirens, as annoying as they might be, always pass and dim, these were only getting louder and shriller.

"It must be some thriller they are filming," he concluded at last. "But since when is all of L.A. an extension of Hollywood?" he wondered ruefully.

Rami went back to contemplating the useless shaver in his hand when his attention was yanked elsewhere. He had come to Tinsel Town to sell Judaica and work on customer relations, not to be embroiled in the middle of an action film. Yet right outside his door he heard the likes of a platoon racing down the hall, and when he turned toward the window, there were actors in full firefighter regalia scaling the tip of a truck-mounted extension ladder at an alarming clip — converging on his room with their axes extended, like lancers galloping for the kill! But Rami wasn't wearing any armor, quite the opposite.

"Leave it to the Americans to make acting look so frightfully real," Rami thought to himself, in no way enjoying the show. The axes were coming too close for comfort — his own and that of the precious antiques he had placed adjacent to the window. He was just about to approach the actors and in his best director's poise gesticulate, "CUT!" when his door was assaulted by either a battering ram or a nuclear attack, he wasn't sure which.

Before he knew it, four firefighters had broken in to his room, joining two more who came crashing through the window. Etzioni was frozen, nay, paralyzed by an acute case of the screaming meemies.

"Where's the smoke coming from?" he

was asked at least five times by he knew not how many men. But Etzioni could not find his tongue and meekly raised his hands, cringing in full submission.

"Looks clean, Chris," one of the firefighters who scanned the room reported to his senior.

The chief looked at the terrified hotel guest in his underwear and at last offered, "Sorry, buddy," motioning at the same time for the troops to withdraw.

After the last debacle, the LAFD knew they had to be on the scene in no time — or at least, before the television crews. This time they managed to beat their nemesis, but not by much. On the heels of the retreating firemen, reporters, light crews and sound grips filled Rami's room. Deft at their work, before a protest could even be uttered, they captured — in living color — scantily clad Etzioni wearing nothing but his tank top and shorts and clutching the offending shaver in his hand.

THAT EVENING roughly 9.5 million television viewers were treated to an exposé of Rami Etzioni. The clip started wide, taking in the smashed windows and shards of glass glittering like jewels amid samples of Judaica items. It then closed in tightly upon the cause of all the commotion: one Rami Etzioni from Bnei Brak, Israel. The frame covered the shaver in his hand, his rather casual attire and a clock in the background displaying 5:25 in the afternoon, broad daylight on the second day of *Shavuos*.

It was a difficult image to forget, especially as it was the first that many saw when they turned on their sets that night. Etzioni's greatest competitor could never have arranged or paid for such drop-dead advertising.

RAMI'S TRIP was significantly less successful than he had anticipated. His credibility as an observant Jew from Bnei Brak was tarnished and this was reflected in sales.

When he returned back home he made his way to Kleiner's and sought out Dr. Berman with his tail between his legs. "When the Rabbis declared that an act may not be performed even *b'chadrei chadorim*," he confessed, "they knew precisely what they were talking about. You would never believe what happened to me; it was one real alarming episode..."

It was an uncharacteristic acknowledgment, but Rami quickly reverted to type. "Hey, Doc," he said, throwing his arm solicitously around his American mentor, "could I interest you in a waaaaay underpriced *Megillah* from the Island of Rhodes? This beaut is authentic, capital A, it will really enhance your Purim like nothing you have e v e r seen in your life before..."

Heard from: Dr. Moshe Brooks

The Broadest Shoulders

*T*ORAH FLOURISHED in Europe during the beginning of the twentieth-century. *Yeshivos* abounded by the scores and our nation was blessed with a multitude of Torah greats, righteous and saintly spiritual giants, including, to name but a few, the Chofetz Chaim, the Ohr Somayach and Reb Chaim Brisker. Yet, everyone would agree that during that time, the heaviest burden of leadership and guidance was assumed by Reb Chaim Ozer Grodzinski of Vilna. The scene in that famed apartment on 17 Zavalna Street defied description until Reb Yaakov

Yitzchak Ruderman, the famed *Rosh Yeshivah* of Ner Israel, came up with an analogy (as related and immortalized by Rabbi Yitzchak Breitowitz) to describe the man sitting at the nerve center of Lithuanian — and quite arguably, world — Jewry.

"Imagine," Rav Ruderman proposed to his spellbound audience, "the chess grandmaster playing sixteen opponents simultaneously. He skirts up and down the table executing strategic moves that inhibit, thwart and stump his opponents, leaving them struggling desperately to extricate themselves."

That was Reb Chaim Ozer's living room, but without the opponents. Instead of moving to inhibit, thwart and stump, Reb Chaim Ozer assisted, encouraged and bolstered those around him, helping them to extricate themselves from their personal problems. In the *gadol hador*'s living room, all would strategize with him, sharing their deepest problems, issues beyond their comprehension and personal matters requiring resolution. The seats at his long table were all occupied by Jews of every stripe and color vying for, and receiving, his attention.

THERE WAS a venerable *rosh yeshivah* who had come to discuss a perplexing Talmudic dilemma and an energetic *gabbai tzedakah* who had a pressing question regarding charity funds. Sitting alongside them was a destitute widow seeking financial assistance to marry off her daughter, while a renowned halachic authority sought Reb Chaim Ozer's attention concerning a novel technological development. A bespectacled young man wanted advice as to which yeshivah would be the best suited for him and a forlorn *yid* needed nothing more than a generous dose of encouragement. Two adversaries — seated at opposite ends of the table — wanted the Rav to settle their dispute, but could barely interrupt the acrimonious jibes they were hurling at one another long enough to explain their arguments to him. One yeshivah official had traveled from afar concerning a curriculum issue, while a communal leader needed guidance regarding the dispensation of Joint Distribution funds. An officious representative from an outlying town was inquiring about the appointment of a kashrus supervisor, and a high-level delegation sought clarification regarding how to conduct themselves in dealings with the civil authorities. A demure young lady wished to know whether she should proceed with a *shidduch*, and an indignant *ba'al habayis* maintained that the *chazzan* in his shul was not mindful of halacha. A prominent businessman was debating investment in a particular venture, but neither he nor his colleagues in the financial world had the proper acumen to assess the pros and cons. A *talmid chacham* toward the end of the table had come to request an approbation for his freshly completed work on the writings of the Rambam, and far closer to the head of the table, *Rebbetzin* Grodzinski, clutching the telephone receiver, relayed a query from an overseas caller.

All the while, Reb Chaim Ozer remained perfectly composed, serenely penning *teshuvos* to the dozens of letters he had received that day. A telegram terminal was located in his very basement, and bundles of cables were brought upstairs hourly. The mail was delivered to his address thrice daily — this was the only way the postal authority could keep up with the volume and spare the mailman's back. If anyone felt that the Rav did not — *could* not — fully understand what he wanted, Reb Chaim

Ozer would repeat what he had said even more clearly than the petitioner had expressed it himself.

Even the chess analogy falls short of describing the scene: try to picture the energy, the decibel-level, the conflict, the vies for attention and the sheer pandemonium that were a constant. And, of course, Rav Chaim Ozer's ever-present equanimity.

REB CHAIM OZER would leave his residence for weeks on end, directing the rescue of thousands of starving refugees during WWI and collecting funds and organizing committees to care for the war victims. In the interbellum period, he was directly responsible for the resettling of Jews from countless communities in war-ravished Europe.

Not only had Reb Chaim Ozer succeeded Reb Yitzchak Elchanon as the paramount scholar-respondent-statesman of the Orthodox world, he surpassed his predecessor in terms of the leadership that he exerted in all facets of Jewish life. His dynamic guidance was most manifest in his direction of the rehabilitation of the Jewish communities after WWI and his spear heading of rescue activities during WWII. Though exhausted and ill, the frail septuagenarian never faltered in taking charge of the crucial rescue work. His devoted student in America, Rabbi Eliezer Silver, created the American branch of the Va'ad Hatzolah.* In February, 1940, Rabbi Silver decided to dispatch his devotee, Dr. Samuel Schmidt, to report on the situation in Europe and coordinate the *Vaad*'s activities with Reb Chaim Ozer.

If ever there was an odd-couple, it was Rabbi Silver and Dr. Schmidt. Both were born in Lithuania, but there the similarities ended. Rabbi Silver arrived in America, already a married man, having studied under Reb Chaim Ozer for several years. Dr. Schmidt came from a non-religious background and immigrated to the United States at the age of twelve. He studied in M.I.T. and then moved to Cincinnati where he worked for B'nai Brith and founded a local Jewish weekly, *Every Friday*.

---

* Emergency Committee for War-Torn *Yeshivos* that was established originally to rescue rabbis and yeshivah students with the outbreak of WWII. It was broadened to assist all European Jews with the revelation of the Final Solution.

It is a tribute to Rabbi Eliezer Silver's magnetic personality that a secular Jewish thinker, who idolized socialism, would regard him in such high esteem. Rabbi Silver's hold over the man was so pervasive that when the Rabbi asked him to depart for war-ravaged Europe, he did so without hesitation.

When Schmidt arrived in Vilna, he made his way, as did untold others, to 17 Zavalna Street to seek information. By this point, none of the questions posed to the outstanding Sage of the generation were academic — each and every one was a matter of life and death. Poland was undergoing ghettoization and in a matter of weeks, Western Europe would fall to the Nazis. For every Jew in Europe, the German noose was pulling inexorably tighter.

Reb Chaim Ozer was deathly ill, suffering from terminal cancer. Somehow, he still had a smile for everyone; his countenance was gaunt, yet radiant. The scholar was confined to bed, which meant that he received just as many people as before, but instead of sitting at his table, he was prostrate on a mattress in the parlor.

In a room packed with Torah scholars and religious refugees, Dr. Schmidt stood out like a winter coat at the beach. But, like his fellow brethren, he, too, had entered that hallowed home with life-and-death questions — on a communal, rather than a personal level.

When Dr. Samuel Schmidt approached Reb Chaim Ozer, the *gadol* gently placed his withered hand upon his visitor's shoulder. "Do you mind," the venerable Rabbi asked reverently, "if I refer to you as *Reb Shmuel?*" "Reb" is the traditional, though very minor title of respect, perhaps akin to referring to a teenager as "young man."

"Oh, I... I am hardly worthy of that title!" Schmidt demurred. But Reb Chaim Ozer's gentle hand was still touching Schmidt's shoulder and his warm eyes were fixed on his guest, indicating that it was, indeed, appropriate. "If you only knew..." Schmidt was about to say, but Rabbi Grodzinski didn't let him get that far.

"You are indeed worthy — very worthy of the title — for having left the security of the United States to travel to a war zone in aid of your brethren. Reb Shmuel," the Rabbi sonorously pronounced, invoking time-honored wisdom of the ages and voluminous Talmudic scholarship, "the title is truly most befitting."

In a dispatch written for *Every Friday*, Schmidt reflected how at that moment, a metamorphosis occurred. Dr. Samuel Schmidt, the secular, Jewish nationalist, had transformed into Reb Shmuel, an observant, Jewish activist.

IN A MOMENT, Reb Chaim Ozer had changed a life. And Reb Shmuel was just one of countless individuals who were privileged to come under the influence of the Rav's caring demeanor. When Reb Shmuel departed to return to the United States, he carried Rabbi Grodzinski's letter of thanks to his wife. Despite the frail Rav's myriad duties and life-saving efforts, he did not forget to commend Mrs. Schmidt for allowing her husband to sail on his dangerous mission of compassion.

The *gadol hador* knew how to thank and he knew how to encourage; enervation and disease didn't make the slightest difference.

Though that may be a bold assertion, the following anecdote is a bold substantiation.

AT THAT VERY TIME, while Vilna was teeming with thousands of refugees, and hunger, squalor and fear were everywhere, all eyes turned to Reb Chaim Ozer for direction. The Sage's body was racked with torturous pain, but he would not allow painkillers to be purchased when the money could be used to feed the starving.

Reb Chaim Ozer's deteriorating health did nothing to diminish the number of people seeking his counsel. On one particular day, he saw the usual fare of rabbis, communal leaders, widows, yeshivah students, the downcast and the confused. There were also a bride and groom. Even with a catastrophic refugee situation, numerous exiled *yeshivos* searching for roofs over their heads and countless orphans with no one to fend for them, Reb Chaim Ozer still had time to bless a couple about to be wed. But that is not all.

The couple related to the Sage that they were the only ones from their families to make it to the relative safety of Vilna. They knew nothing about their parents' plights, nor did they have any relatives to escort them to the *chuppah*. All they asked was that the Rabbi bless them.

Reb Chaim Ozer's tremendous heart went out to this couple and he inquired as to whether the bride had studied the laws of family purity. The young lady did not respond; instead she lowered her head in embarrassment. "Do not be ashamed, my daughter," Reb Chaim Ozer soothed in a fatherly tone. "Surely, if you would be at home, your mother would have taught you these laws, or she would have arranged for a teacher to impart the intricacies of this mitzvah, the very essence of Judaism."

Mirrored on the bride's face was the tragedy of the times. Instead of preparing with joyful anticipation for what should have been the happiest day of her life, she was approaching that day amidst anguish and ignorance. But at least about this second problem there was something that the Rav could do. Personally.

WITHOUT hesitating even a second, Reb Chaim Ozer pulled himself out of bed and requested permission from the groom to speak privately with the *kallah* for a few minutes — a nigh impossibility in that crowded apartment. Of course the young man acceded.

The venerable Rabbi and the young woman walked to the window where they could not be overheard. And there, for the next half hour, the *gadol hador* stared fixedly outside as he patiently and methodically explained the pertinent laws. When the lesson was over (and his body spent) Reb Chaim Ozer collapsed back into his bed.

The towering scholar then summoned all of his resources to fervently bless the couple that they be privileged to build an everlasting house in Israel. He presented them with a cash gift in honor of the occasion and turned to his wife to request that she attend the wedding on his behalf.

And then, without a moment's respite, he immediately turned to the next person on line.

Based on: an article in the May-June 1967 issue of *Jewish Life* by Rabbi Aaron Rakeffet

Beautiful

Totally Awesome

ASSISTANT PRINCIPAL Mrs. Nechama Landesman had the fine art of Shabbaton-planning down to a science. Or so she thought.

Parental permission slips: check. Health forms and medication lists: check. Room-assignments: check. Copious quantities of food and drink: check.

Mrs. Landesman, like only the most gifted educators, understood that high-school students are like crashing rivers insisting on their natural course. No matter how worrisome — even potentially disastrous — the course, they can't be made to flow in the opposite direction.

She knew that the best thing to do with a river, is build a city alongside it. This is why she was gathering up her students from the Yeshiva University High School for Girls (YULA) of Los Angeles to hold their annual Shabbaton in a campsite overlooking the Pacific coast. It would have been a lot easier — and certainly a lot cheaper, for a perennially strapped yeshivah to conduct a Shabbaton in the city, but hosting a retreat out in the rugged California hinterland was a statement that the school wished to make to its students. The message read: Torah study and religious observance are not confined to the parameters of the school campus. Torah is everywhere. It is in the heart and it is in the mind, in the sacred and the everyday, in the urban classroom and in the windswept wilderness.

Every teacher who participated in the retreat was assigned a role and Mrs. Landesman was in charge of the overall organization. And if the catering supplies, sleepingquartersand*eiruv*werenotheadache-inducing enough, she also took it upon herself to provide a special surprise for the eight girls who, as it happened, had birthdays that weekend.

River-tamer Nechama Landesman always liked to think big, to go the extra mile. Accordingly, she ordered two over-the-top gorgeous, industrial-sized birthday cakes to enable the entire school to share in the celebration with an equal dose of sugar-shock.

So it was on a normal, crazy, busy Friday morning that Mrs. Landesman, before heading out to the Malibu Mountains, was off to the bakery to pick up the cakes. But the errand took much longer than expected. One of the cakes was prepared, as per her careful instructions, with four names in pink-and- yellow frosting, written in curlicues and set between frosted *fleurs de lis*, sugary petal tips and flowers finely etched of frosting.

The second cake: nada.

Oh, the flowers and fondant were pretty

enough. But the names had not been added. Because it was *erev Shabbos* and she still had so much to oversee, she might have forgone some other shortcoming of Cake #2. But not the names. This mistake could be misconstrued as favoritism; it could foster secret hurts and festering jealousies. It was a worth a simple investment of time to preempt these problems.

However, the task proved to be anything but simple; and there wasn't much time. The cake-designer was not on the premises. "You don't need to be a baker or a cake-designer to do this," Mrs. Landesman protested. "If you give me the gizmo, *I* can do it."

"That's the problem," said the woman behind the counter apologetically. "The baker who does our lettering," and then her voice dropped to a barely audible tone, "likes to think that he is the only one who can do it, even though he really knows better. That's why he locks up his pastry decorating bags, sculpting spatulas and icing molds when he is away. Yeah, I know it sounds weird, but I guess if you got up at four in the morning to frost cakes and no one ever associates you with the product you also might act kooky. As a matter of fact, he used to sign 'Ramiro' under his artwork, like he was Rembrandt or something, until the owner told him to cut it out..."

Nechama actually started to feel sorry for the guy, but was more concerned about getting to the retreat nice and early. "When do you expect him back?" she asked hopefully.

"I'd say about a quarter-of-an-hour, but no guarantees."

Mrs. Landesman weighed her scant options which included taking the cake across town to a different kosher bakery. Not only would this request (to decorate a cake that was baked elsewhere) be a bit awkward — driving to the other bakery would take at least fifteen minutes. Even if they were able to fix the cake immediately, it would set her back almost a half-hour.

She was torn. How could she fète half of the birthday girls and ignore the others? She considered having the other four names scraped off, but realized that this would make the first cake look like birds had pecked at it. It really was worth waiting, but who knew if Ramiro would return in fifteen minutes, or, *chas v'challilah, mañana...*

Still, her inner voice echoed ominously that on an *erev Shabbos*, it was best not to delay, especially as she had a long drive ahead of her. At the time of the birthday celebration she would turn on the charm and apologize profusely for the unwitting omission.

Reluctantly, she left the bakery and began her journey. Because of the morning events she was already running late, but Mrs. Landesman didn't fret for *there was still PLENTY of time before Shabbos.* Furthermore, she had been apprised of a shortcut to the campsite that would save valuable time.

Author's note: "There was still plenty of time before Shabbos," dear reader, is the classic set-up. Like when the innocent protagonist goes up the creaky stairs in the horror film to investigate the bewildering noise. What will happen in the next scene is a mystery, but it's safe to say it wasn't just "the wind." Perhaps you have an idea by now where this is leading...

AND SO Nechama Landesman made her way through the mountainside at Calabassas en route to the mountains of Malibu where she would connect with the Pacific Coast Highway, otherwise known as California Highway 1, and even better known as one of America's premiere scenic drives. Every few miles reveals a different scene of picture-postcard perfection, from rugged ocean cliffs and pounding surf to nature preserves and picturesque rural towns. The road is hugged by sandy beaches, rocky bluffs, idyllic coves with roaring surf, tide pools and lagoons.

Mrs. Landesman could not help but be distracted by the magnificent views. Natural archways carved in the cliffs by the sea, frolicking sea lions and otters are not everyday sights, even in "So Cal" — so she must be forgiven for having driven so many miles without having spotted the turn-off for the retreat.

But scenery aside, and it truly was on every side, she realized with a start that it was getting very late. The problem was that getting off at the wrong exit was never an easily rectifiable mistake on the Pacific Coast Highway. The area is deserted, wild terrain and the wrong turn could land you anywhere, making it challenging to get back to where you started. There was no one to ask, and no convenience stores or gas stations along the way.

Because of the lateness of the hour, Mrs. Landesman began to increase her speed on the winding, one-lane-in-each-direction road, and took every turn-off that appeared promising. However, every exit to the right sent her back to the valley and every exit to the left deposited her literally on the beach. *Time seems to fly the fastest when you are headed nowhere...*

Desperate people do desperate things. The road had no shoulder that would allow a driver to pull over and flag down a passing vehicle. To the right of the road was impenetrable mountain, and to the left was a terrifying, breathtakingly steep cliff. There was no way to pass *a car up ahead* — not as if this were a practical consideration — without fully occupying the oncoming lane.

But, as noted, desperation is the great motivator, and careful, cautious Nechama Landesman stopped her car smack-dab in the middle of California Highway 1, put on her flashing hazard-lights, waited, and prayed for a Shabbos miracle. The great orb that was the sun had already positioned itself to the west over the horizon and was preparing to take a dive into the ocean. On any other day, it would have been an awe-inspiring sight.

As Nechama tensely awaited salvation every second felt like a minute, and every minute was an agonizing hour. She was sure that she could actually see the sun inching lower, and the sight was exquisite agony. Mercifully, she heard a car approaching around the bend and her hopes surged.

EVEN in her frazzled state, Nechama could have have dealt with a studio head in a Lamborghini, or a cross-country trucker wielding his heavy rig, for after all, this was California. But she was rendered totally speechless by the cacophonous jalopy that shuddered to a stop before her. The ramshackle VW bug was a mind-blowing blast from the groovy Sixties past — from its neon, customized paint job of multi-colored swirls and paisley and flower-power blossoms, to the strange burps being emitted by its vintage muffler.

The bumper stickers, occupying far more real estate than just the bumpers, were a fair indication of who might be behind the wheel. "Retro" didn't even scratch the surface. The hippie mantras "Peace Now" "Save the Planet" "No Nukes!" and the classic, "Make Love, Not War" spoke volumes — not to mention Abbie Hoffman's slogan plastered on the hood: "Avoid all needle drugs. The only dope worth shooting is Richard Nixon."

The car looked dazed and confused, tie-dyed and re-used, and it had a lotta mileage on it. And so did the twosome who inhabited the front seats.

When the driver opened his door the heavy metal of Jimi Hendrix echoed into the California canyons. Out lumbered a corpulent fellow in patched denim overalls who could only be described as middle-aged if he would be lucky enough to make it to 120. With a steady breeze blowing up from the shore, the man's long, greying tresses were *blowin' in the wind,* and strands of Indian beads and feathers encircled his deeply-lined neck. The dude looked like he had just driven in from the Summer of Love. And it was obvious to Nechama, as she cringed with apprehension, that he didn't look particularly pleased to have been stopped in the middle of the highway while he was chasing his bliss...

At this point his female companion also wafted from the vehicle; and although clearly wilted by the passage of years, she too was fixed in time as the quintessential "flower child," her barefoot feet still firmly planted, metaphorically of course, in the mud of Woodstock. And she also didn't appear thrilled about being forced to pull over. The two approached, and Nechama felt a small knot of fear raging uncontrollably in her stomach.

She wanted to wave a meek, floppy "hi" but she was too unnerved, she realized, to move. She had learned the term "disconnect" in a psychology course and sought to apply it, but in vain; the situation was too complicated, the wild cards were too many, and everything was just too surreal. She had no idea where she was, Shabbos was imminent, her head was beginning to throb, and her only way out of her predicament was to put herself in the hands of these trippy Sonny and Cher look-alikes, whose lovemobile was now blasting mutant girl-group oohings, synthesized disco-funk horns, and cheesy fuzz-guitar squawks.

Joe-Hippie was closing in on Mrs. Landesman now; in three feet he would be in striking range...

"Peace!" he called out to Nechama, spreading his chubby fingers, and a hint of a smile appeared on his lips. Jane-Hippie, whose every step was accentuated by the high-pitched ringing of bells on her ankle-bracelet, also flashed the peace-sign and extended a flower (which turned out, on closer inspection, to be a dandelion) to Nechama.

Dazedly, Nechama resumed breathing. She had not seen a scene the likes of this one in many, many years. Was she... California Dreamin'?

"Um, totally awesome peace to you, brother and sister," said girls' yeshivah assistant principal Landesman, trying to sound like their, well, *landsman*. But with that she had exhausted her full repertoire of cool lingo. And now that she was over her initial shock of encountering the Electric Kool-Aid Acid Testers, her critical mission returned to center-stage, where it belonged. "I am looking for a campsite," she pressed, urgency very apparent in her tone, "that I just cannot find... and I am incredibly, incredibly rushed..."

Joe-Hippie said he knew where the camp site was and he reckoned that it was about 40 minutes away. As he offered this guesstimate, the sun seemed to drop another two inches in the sky. "Look, um, guys," Nechama began tentatively, "my Sabbath is just about to begin and, like, once that happens I won't be able to drive; that is, I'll be stuck where ever I am when the sun goes down. So, like, don't bother with directions because I *have* directions and they sound just like your directions, and I've been driving up and down this road, like, forever, and I just keep getting more lost..."

"WHOA, THAT IS SO NOT COOL," declared Joe-Hippie.

"SOOOO not cool," Jane-Hippie agreed, shaking her head.

Nechama took a deep breath. "Ummm... I know this sounds crazy, but I, er, need the biggest favor in the world from you. Could you — I mean, would you — be able to drive me to the camp site in my car — I mean in both of our cars?"

Joe and Jane looked at each other quizzically. Nechama suddenly realized they were thinking that *she* was the trippy one.

Unfazed, she continued: "This way I'll be able to go as far as time allows before I have to get out of the car. Look, I know this sounds crazy, and I realize I am asking you to go out of your way... but I'm kinda desperate. *Majorly* desperate.

"Say no more, sister... I know what you are talking about," said Jane-Hippie authoritatively. "I once worked for a man who was Orthodox-Jewish... really great guy. The dude left work early every Friday, you know, to do his Sabbath thing, go to services, be with his family..."

"Wow, that is righteous, babe," said Joe approvingly. "Like, too beautiful..."

"So what are we waiting for, dude?" Jane announced. "Let's take this lady... to do the Sabbath thing!"

NECHAMA'S deflated emotions were suddenly surging. Joe climbed back into an incense-redolent vehicle as YULA's assistant principal handed her car keys to the total stranger in *her* driver's seat. Once they were moving she dared to be hopeful, although she had absolutely no idea how the story would end. At least, consolation-wise, she was finally headed in the right direction.

Nechama hoped that she would be able to prevail upon Joe and Jane to notify those in the campsite not to fret about her, and that they should send out the cavalry *motza'ei Shabbos* on a mission of rescue.

Although everything about the hip-pies bespoke "slo-mo," they devoted them-selves assiduously to getting Nechama to her destination as quickly as possible. Joe knew the highways and the byways, the old roads and the new roads, the side roads and the almost roads, and used all of them and more, to transport his hitchhiker from the Sabbath-observant galaxy to her destination in record time.

Finally, as the road became dotted with signs and arrows for the campsite, Nechama could not stop thanking her driver.

Jane pooh-pooh'ed it with the flick of a heart-tattooed wrist. "Instant karma," she told Nechama calmly. "We believe in doing a 'random act of kindness' for a stranger, when it's your birthday — that's kinda like our religion... and today is my dude's birthday!"

"Would you believe that we were driving around, like, looking for something we could do... and then we were, like, blessed to run into you? Awesome," Jane warbled moving her head from side to side as if she were picking up voices from the wind.

"Awesome," echoed Nechama, without a shred of cynicism.

"It's more than that," Jane added, and her breathy voice took on a serious tone. "This isn't just *any* birthday. My guy, he had cancer. He wasn't supposed to have another birthday. But he beat it... he's a survivor. So this is, like, the birthday of birthdays!"

Nechama's eyes swam with tears and she struggled to find the right words, as the car pulled into the campsite, not more than one minute before sunset. Suddenly they were surrounded by sixty cheering girls, who sprinted over as fast as their long skirts would allow them, to surround their beloved teacher.

One after another, they called out in glee: "Mrs. Landesman! You made it!!"

"With a little help from my friends," she quipped, wondering if they were too young to get the reference (now that she was on a rock & roll-roll.) "And a ton of help from *Hashem!*"

And then, with Joe's help, she managed to unload the equipment for "Shabbaton central" with lightning speed. Parental permission slips: check. Health forms and medication lists: check. Room-assignments: check. Copious quantities of food and drink: check.

Birthday cakes: check.

Mrs. Landesman held onto the bulky cakebox for a moment, staring at the massive sheet-cake through the cellophane window. "Looks like God meant for you to have a mega-incredible birthday today," she said to Joe Hippie, whose face shone with amazement and delight as she handed him the box. "Actually, it looks like this cake has your name on it..."

"I can't believe this!" he chortled. "This is awesome!"

"Totally," said Nechama.

And with that, the two kindly strangers drove slowly into the sunset, and the yeshivah girls and their teachers dove hurriedly into their Shabbos, and it was very, very sweet indeed.

Heard from: Nechama Landesman

The World According to Abe

*W*HAT'S in a name?

Our Sages tell us that it carries the definition of an individual — the key to his personality, his heart, his soul, his potential, even his destiny.

Take the name of the patriarch Avraham ("Abraham," in English). Because of the life he led, the very name bespeaks a courageous love of God, a deep love of his fellow man, and a seminal influence that would change history.

It was the perfect name for a modern-day Jewish leader known to so many simply as "Abe." Dr. Abraham Chames, *z"tl*, a man whom the Chofetz Chaim *Rosh Yeshivah* called "the *gadol hador* in *chessed*," was a giant of a man, in stature and in character, in personality and in deeds. A name synonymous with kindness, generosity, hospitality and humility, and with an unabashedly joyful eagerness to carry out *Hashem*'s will.

Dr. Chames' primary calling was to reach out to those who had been dealt with harshly by life, and wherever possible he tried to get others to do the same. This was, he passionately believed, the most appropriate way to serve God.

His own service was embodied in the clarion call of the Shema, "*b'chol nafshechah uv'chol me'odecha*": "(And you shall love the Lord your God) with all your soul and all your resources." Why, asks the Gemara (*Berachos* 54a), does it say "with all of your resources," if it already says "with all of your soul?" The Talmud answers: "Should there be a man who values his life more than his money, it tells him, '*with all of your soul.*' And should there be a man who values his money more than his life, it tells him *'with all of your resources.'"*

Indeed, there are those who value their time at a premium, and who would prefer to donate money to perform a good deed. Others will volunteer their time to facilitate what is needed, rather than dipping into their resources. Many people, overwhelmed by the pressures of modern life, do neither. Abe — constantly, tirelessly and joyfully — did *both*.

"The World According to Abe" is a step-by-step primer in the fine art of doing — of *living* — *mitzvos*... but beautifully, oh so beautifully! Doctors learned to be better doctors by observing Abe (who was trained as a physician but provided comfort, healing and hope at the helm of a Florida-based medical supply company). Business executives learned how to reap the rewards of professional success without making an idol of those rewards (as in sacrificing ethics or foregoing philanthropy in the name of profit). Rabbis learned to be better shepherds of their flocks (because hubris and ego are the enemies of true leadership and community-building). By watching Abe, we all learned to be better human beings. Because that was what Abe embodied, and what his life celebrated: the humanity in all of us — and the Godliness we mirror, at our very best.

"The World According to Abe" is best revealed through the stories of those he helped. Why? This is a man who would have loathed paeans to his personality or odes to his character. Outgoing, exuberant and open, he was an "in-your-face" presence, but it was never All About Abe.

It was *always* About the Mitzvah.

"The World According to Abe"

❀ **FEEL SOMEONE ELSE'S PAIN AS YOUR OWN AND YOU WILL BE TRULY MOTIVATED TO RELIEVE IT**

Jenny became diabetic so rapidly that she all but missed the warning signs. Seemingly overnight, her body was unable to process the glucose in her blood. She was drained of energy, her thirst was unquenchable, her vision became blurry, and she was afflicted with an alarming numbness in her hands and feet.

The situation was devastating, but she knew exactly where to turn: Dr. Abe Chames. No, he could not effect a medical miracle, though his knowledge of medicine was prodigious. What was in the realm of the extraordinary was the lengths to which he would go for a person in need. If you needed him, he was there for you. Everything else was commentary.

Because Dr. Chames was a partner in a medical supply company, it was assumed — and he never did anything to dispel the rumor (in fact, he *encouraged* it) — that he could supply people with whatever equipment they required... gratis. And so, from the day that Jenny first solicited his assistance to help her monitor her disease, Abe provided her with a glucometer and regular deliveries of test strips.

After Dr. Chames' death, Jenny brought these items to show his partner in the business, in the hope that he would be able to continue providing them.

"For how long was he sending you this equipment?" he asked Jenny, with puzzlement evident in his voice.

"Since the onset of my illness," she replied. "I'd say nearly 20 years."

The man let out a low whistle. "Why, we haven't carried these items in ten years!"

"*What?*" Jenny gasped.

"At least ten years, maybe more! You too have been 'had' by Abe Chames. You thought that he was doing you a tiny favor — practically nothing out of his own pocket — when in fact he was performing an enormous act of kindness, all at his own expense."

৪ ANTICIPATE — DO NOT SIMPLY RESPOND TO — THE NEEDS OF OTHERS

It was just a flash, really. The flash of a worn-out sole of a shoe. Abe spotted it sitting across from a yeshivah high school teacher of his acquaintance. And it bothered Abe... a lot.

A worn-out sole, a tattered skirt, threadbare pants — frankly, these are things that many of us may note in passing, but they registered in a different way for Abe Chames. For if Abe ever saw or intuited a need — and his antennae were always up in this regard — he was determined to fill it.

Abe saw more than just a worn shoe, that afternoon. In that shoe he also saw an old, unreliable car, a house in need of repair, a pile of bills, meals that were scrimped together, family vacations that were wishful thinking. In that shoe, he saw the unmet needs of one of the most valuable and important resources of every Jewish community: its teachers. Abe struggled with how to address that need and consulted with Rabbi Edward Davis from the Young Israel of Hollywood. As always, Rabbi Davis had the perfect solution: "Just like there are bonuses in the business world that are never viewed as acts of charity, we should also institute a similar policy."

Abe took it from there, and on the spot a fund to ease the burdens and enhance the dignity of the yeshivah's teaching staff was created, which became a yearly Pesach project. The *rebbeim* felt as humbled accepting this largesse as an office worker does at receiving a yearly bonus. Abe's dominant involvement in the project forced the hands of many far more affluent than he to give handsomely. This was but one of many such initiatives that Abe quietly launched and oversaw.

❀ WHEN YOU ENCOUNTER A MITZVAH OPPORTUNITY NEVER TARRY; VIEW OTHERS' NEEDS AS YOUR OWN EMERGENCY

For young Micha, it was a trauma that transcended the physical: leaving the only home he had ever known. The soldiers (*his* soldiers), the billy-clubs, the screaming. During the forced evacuation of the Amona settlement in the West Bank, he suffered a number of injuries, including a broken nose. His nose was surgically repaired and repositioned, but the boy was warned that, for at least a year, he must not play sports or even dance in a crowded room for fear of re-injuring the delicate area.

How did the news of an injured, trau-
matized boy make its way half-way around
the world, to Abe Chames in Florida? Abe
was connected to all things Jewish and he
felt a profound sense of responsibility to all
Jews everywhere.

Soon after, Micha's family received a
package labeled "Purim Mask": a sturdy
nose-guard that would enable the boy to
resume every boy's normal activities without fear. And indeed, he wore it on Purim
when he danced exuberantly with his yeshivah — just as the good doctor ordered.

❀ **ALWAYS MAKE THE RECIPIENTS OF A FAVOR
FEEL LIKE THEY ARE THE ONES WHO ARE DO-
ING SOMETHING VERY SPECIAL FOR YOU**

The day-school principal was new on the
job, and though he had certainly *heard* of
Dr. Abe Chames... he really didn't know
what he was in for that afternoon that Abe
came to call. Abe's concern for every Jewish
educational institution for miles around
was so immense, that it extended even to

schools with which neither he nor his children had any personal connection.

Abe was aware that the educator's father had recently passed away, and expressed his condolences as the two men toured the building. In the *beis medrash,* Abe noticed that *krias haTorah* was being performed on a regular metal school desk that had been recruited for the purpose. "Rabbi," Dr. Chames declared, "I'm going to commission an appropriate *shulchan* for the school, in memory of your father."

As the initial shock of Abe's most generous and touching announcement began wearing off, the principal instantly understood what made this man the rare individual he was: Abe both assimilated information and acted upon it immediately. He didn't employ a "to-do" list, for he awarded highest priority to every project he took on. He immediately engaged a carpenter to come to the school and meet with the principal.

When the carpenter arrived, he unfurled his tape-measure, pulled a well-used pencil from behind his ear, took several measurements and rendered a preliminary sketch. As the man was about to leave, the principal inquired, simply out of curiosity, what the cost of such a table might be. The craftsman replied that Dr. Chames had instructed him to use only the finest wood, and that they had agreed upon a price of $2,500.

Flabbergasted, the principal quickly phoned his new benefactor. "Dr. Chames, I... I... don't know what to say," he gasped. "I mean, I'm new here, and you and I, why, we hardly know each other! This table you have arranged for — I am immensely touched and grateful... but it is far too costly! A table can be built out of pine for less than *half* the price..."

"Nuthin' doin', Rabbi!" Abe thundered into the receiver. "A *shulchan* in your father's memory *must* be made of the best materials, and the price is fine. And *please:* this craftsman really, *really* needs the money, and you will be doing me a HUGE favor, by enabling me to help him out!"

The dumbstruck principal quietly returned the telephone receiver to its cradle, digesting his first* taste of what many Jewish educators in South Florida knew to be a routine encounter with the inimitable Dr. Chames.

This was invariably his modus operandi: Making you believe you were doing him an *enormous* favor, instead of the other way around. Maybe, just maybe, because his purity of heart was so great that he really believed it was so.

✿ PERSONAL CONVENIENCE OR EVEN PERSONAL TRAGEDY DOES NOT ABSOLVE YOU FROM CARING FOR OTHERS AS A PRIORITY

Abe Chames arrived at the airport, bound for Israel, lugging with him enough baggage for a small army or a month-long stay at a resort. But, as usual, it wasn't all about Abe; Abe was, as usual, a man on a mission. He regularly sent medical equipment

---

* There was a standard quip in the Miami area that the foreign *meshulach* whose first stop in America was Abe Chames was to be pitied. The naïve fund solicitor would be in for a major let down, optimistically believing that *everyone* in America was as generous as Abe.

to *Hatzolah* in Jerusalem, equipment that was vital for their life-saving work. On this occasion, he decided to provide his unique brand of "Special Delivery," by taking it to the Holy Land himself.

What few people knew, as they observed the big man with the big pile of luggage, was that his heart carried an even heavier burden. This was not simply a standard overseas jaunt for Abe. He was traveling that day to bury his beloved mother in Israel. Abe had revered his parents, Yaakov and Chana Chames, *z"l*; he was the son of Holocaust survivors and he never forgot this for even an instant. In fact, though born in the Midwest (Minneapolis) he loved sounding like he had just come off the boat himself and delighted in quoting *Yiddishisms* from his parents (though, ironically, he never seemed to get American expressions exactly right). Abe valued his humble beginnings as a son of refugees; his business was neither an inheritance nor a windfall but the result of an abundance of hard work and Godly Providence. He assumed no ego and took zero pride from this. The greatest compliment that you could give him was to call him a "greener."

It was in the *zechus* of his mother, to bless her memory, that he elected to transport the bulky equipment to Israel that day — placing the needs of others ahead of his own, even in the midst of this most sorrowful journey.

He would be in Israel for fewer than twelve hours.

❀ THERE IS NO CONCEPT OF YOTZEI WHEN IT COMES TO CHESSED; "THIS IS NOT MY LINE/ IN MY REPERTOIRE/IN MY CATALOGUE" IS NOT A DEFERMENT

Abe was well aware that many local doctors and businessmen were not adequately being *koveah ittim* so he decided to do his small share in this regard. Specifically, he began hosting a one-hour *shiur* ending with 10 minutes of *mussar* every Tuesday evening.

As with every project he embarked upon, his wife Deborah was his full partner. In this instance, her role was probably *more* than 50%, for there was no question that many of the *shiur*-attendees came for the delicious spread of snacks that she always provided.

The *shiur* grew in popularity, but after its founder's attendance became sporadic because of his frequent business trips, it no longer made sense for Abe to host the *shiur*. He saw to it that it would continue in a different venue. And in classic Chames style, he did a lot more than that.

He acquired two sturdy metal lockers to house the *sefarim* and the refreshments he stocked for the weekly class. The gastronomic accompaniment was nothing less than what he would have at his own table, and indeed far more — though he no longer hosted the *shiur* nor attended it.

As commonplace as it is, even second nature to generous and magnanimous individuals, Abe totally and thoroughly rejected the concept of "*yotzei.*" "At what point have I fulfilled my obligation?" was a thought that never crossed his mind. This concept was not only foreign to him, it was an anathema.

Primarily in the realm of *chessed,* but in

fact in every aspect of his life, Abe was always trying to improve on his own actions; he saw opportunities for growth and culled valuable lessons where others didn't see a thing.

❀ THE PERFORMANCE OF A KINDNESS IS NEVER FOR RECOGNITION OR REWARD

Dr. Abraham Chames invariably sat in the back of the shul, and he would joke that this way no one could see him — for his presence was larger-than-life in every sense of the word. The true reason was that he always did whatever he could to be out of the spotlight. That is why he was so torn when his son's yeshivah repeatedly wished to honor him at its annual dinner.

There is nothing that he liked *less* than being recognized for his panoply of *mitzvos*. But his love of those *mitzvos* and of *tzedakah* — his desire to be of service — was so great, that he was even willing to do something seriously beyond his comfort zone, in order to express his gratitude. In one full sweep he would also be furthering the aims of the school, showing appreciation for the honor, and acting as a role model for others in demonstrating that no one should turn away from any sort of mitzvah.

Whether it was a thousand-watt mitzvah that would illuminate an entire community, or a minor act that brightened just one moment in time for one family, Abe would execute it quietly and graciously. At his shiva, as family and friends and strangers came to pay their respects to the *aveilim,* story after story came to light.

One couple introduced themselves, saying, "you do not know us, as we have never met — nor did we know Dr. Chames..." They were educators, new in town, and soon after their arrival they celebrated the bris of their newborn. As their means were quite limited, the meal they were serving was bare-bones, of the bagels-and-cheese-spread variety. But after the *seudas mitzvah* was spread out on the buffet table, they noticed it included an elegant and delicious French toast dish. When they asked the caterer about the mistake, they were informed there was no mistake. Abe Chames knew that teachers were, for the most part, woefully underpaid; it was one of the great frustrations of his life. And so, where he could, he added what he could. Yes, they were perfect strangers, newcomers to the community. But he wanted their *simcha* to be multiplied and magnified. So he did what he did best: he made it happen.

Everybody lost their benefactor when Abe died — but so few knew! In many instances — probably the majority — the recipients were never aware that Abe Chames as, in fact, the wind beneath their wings. No doubt the students in Yeshivat Shilo, for example, have no idea how much an American from Florida contributed to their education; and Abe would have it no other way.

The irony was, although Abe loved to take full advantage of every possible giving opportunity, he would never make a fuss about himself. He would put himself in orbit to help a stranger, but would demur a thousand times before reluctantly agreeing to accept the tiniest token from someone else. He was appalled at the very notion of calling in a favor.

❀ NEVER INQUIRE PERFUNCTORILY ABOUT SOMEONE'S WELFARE

Sarah is confined to a wheelchair, and like many who live in the world of the disabled, she is often asked by well-intentioned people: "So, how are you?" The sad reality is, however, that few of them actually wait to hear the answer.

Abe Chames was one of those rare few. Not only did he — as a physician, as a mensch — truly *want* to hear the answer; he wanted to hear, so that if there was a problem, he could act. True, the man was the quintessential joker at heart, but his inquiries, especially when he sensed someone may be in trouble or compromised, were the ultimate in sincerity. *"What's new in school?"* he would demand of youths who refused to meet his steady gaze as he waited patiently for their reply. *"Nu, so tell me, what's going on with you?"* he would inquire of those who, for the most part, in the words of the great essayist Thoreau, "lead lives of quiet desperation." For there was absolutely no effort he would spare to alleviate another's suffering.

Sarah confided tearfully that she was in pain from sores due to her seated position. For Abe, this distressing news was nothing less than a full-blown, time-sensitive mandate. His medical supply company did not carry a product geared to Sarah's condition, but in that moment, he knew it *should*. With characteristic urgency, he put himself to the task of finding the best possible solution to Sarah's problem, and he discovered a specially-designed cushion that was just what the doctor ordered... so he ordered it (with expedited service, *k'darko*). And with characteristic generosity, he did not charge for it; why, he wouldn't dream of it!

Some months later, Sarah was a guest in the Chames home, and used the opportunity to thank Abe profusely for providing this life-saver — so indispensable, she exclaimed, that she used it at home *and* at work. Abe interrupted with a gasp: "I can't believe you shlep that thing every day back and forth to work!"

Two business days later, a second cushion was delivered to Sarah's doorstep. Of course, there was no note attached.

❀ TREAT THOSE WHO NEED YOUR HELP AS IF THEY WERE YOUR OWN CHILDREN

Abe's concern for *rebbeim*, especially those affiliated with the local yeshivah, was all-encompassing. He knew the challenges of their lives and strove to be of service to them. A tattered coat — and a rebbe would have something better, as soon as Abe could provide it. He bankrolled their yeshiva paychecks, gave them special help for Pesach and even arranged a personal trainer as he was concerned for their wellness, too.

And, as much *kavod* and practical support as he gave the yeshivah's educators, he gave its secretaries and support staff as well. To many people, these workers were invisible — but not to Abe Chames. He had a fiercely loyal respect for his fellow man, no matter his (or her) station in life. He reached out to all: from exalted yeshivah instructors to unsung secretaries, hospital personnel to housekeepers, toll collectors to trash collectors. His purity of heart was such that he saw — and responded to — the Godliness in each individual.

✿ RESPECT THE GOD-GIVEN UNIQUENESS OF EACH INDIVIDUAL BY PERSONALIZING YOUR INQUIRIES, REGARDLESS TO WHOM YOU ARE SPEAKING

When an individual possesses a light-hearted, informal manner, one might view his inquiries as being casual; when this individual knows *many* people, one might see those inquiries as being impersonal. But that was never the case with the always jocular, endlessly popular Abe Chames. He made everybody feel that they were his best friend*; and in a way they were, for the man had no tier distinction in his friendships; he embraced an acquaintance the way he greeted a family member or a life-long friend. When he spoke to you, you were his focus; you had his full attention and you

---

* The first school day after Abe's passing (he passed away suddenly on a Shabbos) the children from the neighborhood were so devastated that a psychologist was called in to offer group grief counseling. Every child asserted that Abe was their best friend. At first the session started to sound a bit absurd and childish ("He was my best friend," "No, he was my best friend!...") until the kids actually found solace and comfort from the fact that he was, indeed, *everyone's* best friend.

were the only person in the world.

Not only were Abe's questions utterly sincere; they were always personalized, reflecting that he was the consummate listener, always up-to-date and monitoring each person's situation... because he really cared. At his son's wedding — when it would surely be understandable to be swept up in all of the "mazel tovs" and "*im-yirzeh-Hashem*-by-you's" — he interrupted the hand-pumping to ask the law student about the bar exam, the new father about the baby, the Jets fan about those Jets. He paused in the whirl of the *simcha*-dancing to ask those who were suffering about their suffering, the infirm about their pain.

Because his questions were not a formality and he cared about the response, countless individuals of all ages and walks of life poured out their hearts to him. He listened to their confidences with endless patience and compassion.

And what was the end-result of these highly emotional, intensely personal interactions? For Abe, it always came down to one thing, the *right* thing. In a word: *action.*

✿ TRULY EFFECTIVE BENEVOLENCE SOMETIMES MEANS THINKING, DOING — AND GIVING — "OUTSIDE THE BOX"

One of the most powerful tools in this Pied Piper's seemingly limitless arsenal of hydraulically-charged pick-me-ups, was a most unusual — as Abe mirthfully referred to it — *"aliyah la'regel"*: Disney World in Orlando, Florida. This is where Abe would send someone who sorely needed a lift, a break, a smile, a reconnection with family, a little "R & R." He presented this gift to people who could never in their wildest dreams afford to take their (sizeable) families on such an exciting junket, like the strapped *rebbeim* and teachers from the yeshivah. Or families in the community who were deeply mired in illness, tragedy or strife. Or those celebrating a special milestone — a birthday, the anniversary of a wedding, or of many years of faithful service in their jobs. Likewise he would treat members of Deborah's staff to Disney perks and would tell anyone from her office (in Miami) who was Orlando-bound to stop at the Chames' house — along the way — to pick up tickets and others perks.

Everyone he sponsored was looked after as his personal guest (whether he was present or not): travel, accommodations, entrance fees and Disney dollars were taken care of, sparing no expense to ensure that this would be the most enjoyable vacation of their lives.

And whenever he got wind of a family that was scheduled to spend only *half* a day in the sprawling constellation of theme parks, Abe knew that it was almost always because they couldn't afford more. So he would, in one way or another, add more, so that they could relax and truly enjoy their visit. He became their program director, food-services supplier and logistical guru. Invariably he would provide far better accommodations and more elaborate meals than one would ever arrange for oneself.

Abe would give (not lend) what he thought would be most useful for the individual pilgrims, from local guide books and *Disney for Dummies* to ice packs and thermal bags — even, one time, a "George Foreman" grill for one *rebbe* and his family so that they would not have to subsist solely on tuna sandwiches. Whatever anyone could conceivably need to enjoy every moment.

During school breaks, when he inevitably sent a number of families to meet Mickey and Minnie, Abe himself was also *"oleh regel"* and shlepped enormous quantities of food in order to host a barbeque-extravaganza as the gastronomic climax to a spectacular day.

Abe knew that for these weary travelers, a Disney vacation meant more than just pictures in an album. These excursions were a balm for stressed-out souls and over-extended families. They generated a precious light and warmth all their own.

The very same Chamesian logic mandated that he purchase diamond earrings as a gift for one of his employees, to commemorate her 20 years of devoted service. It was an extravagant gift, unquestionably, but Abe instinctively felt it was a *necessary* one. The recipient was a single woman who had once been married, decades earlier. She had great difficulty making ends meet and lived from paycheck to paycheck; at one point she was in danger of having her car repossessed and Abe Chames underwrote the cost of the car, eliminating the debt.

He realized that if his gift were to be a check for a few thousand dollars it would quickly disappear. But here was an opportunity to provide her with something that would make her feel truly appreciated, glamorous and feminine. His hunch was spot-on; it always was.

The same finesse graced every project he undertook. It was hallmark, it was legion... it was Abe.

❀ YOUR MINDSET MUST ALWAYS BE: "WHAT CAN I DO FOR OTHERS?"

When a baby was born with cystic fibrosis (a congenital disease causing serious respiratory and digestive problems) in Abe's Hollywood, Florida, community, he took an immediate interest in her and her family's well-being. Whenever he attended a medical equipment trade show, he would invariably return with another nebulizer (breathing apparatus), critical for the care of one afflicted with CF. He took great care to always acquire the ones that were the most child-friendly, and adorned with kiddie themes... and to deliver them personally with the warm and cheerful demeanor that was, in itself, a priceless gift to all those who were beneficiaries of his largesse.

Indeed, wherever and whenever his assistance was sought, or just as likely, if he *perceived* a need, he would undertake to rectify the issue. Whenever someone turned to him with a problem large or small, he would listen intently and reply: "Let me make a few calls."

He always did, and they always bore fruit.

Abe's passion for helping was without ego, without regard to social status. Unlike so many, Abe was happily blind to such matters. A gardener once confided in him that his tools had been stolen, and on the spot Abe gave him $500 to replace them; the cash was a gift, not to be subtracted from his gardening wages.

He treated all workers with affection and — again, that word — respect. He always

provided the gardeners with cold drinks
and a snack. Abe was far more than simply
thoughtful; he served others with unusual
and heartfelt zeal. For if he was home on
a scorching day and he realized his freezer
had run out of ice, Abe would drop everything to make a run to 7/11 so that the gardeners' drinks were refreshing and frosty-
cold.

Is it any wonder, then, that the gardeners came in to pay a heartfelt condolence
call? That the garbage men cried when
they heard of Abe's passing? That the mail
carrier wrote *two* condolence cards?

  IT IS INCUMBENT UPON EVERY JEW TO AWARD
FUND-SOLICITORS THE HIGHEST RESPECT,
FOR WITHOUT THEIR OFT-THANKLESS WORK,
OUR MOST VITAL INSTITUTIONS WOULD FAIL

The principal of a yet another South Florida day school recalled one of the many
occasions when he phoned Dr. Chames to
solicit a journal ad for the school's dinner.
There was absolutely no hard sell required,
for Dr. Chames jumped at the opportunity to purchase a pricey, full-page ad, even

though his children did not attend that school. In fact, the deal was closed before the principal's pitch was even out of his mouth.

The next morning, a parent proudly informed the principal that *she* had solicited a by-no-means-cheap half-page ad from Abe just one day earlier. The principal could not believe his ears. He was all too familiar with the delicate dance of fund raising, of how people reacted to multiple solicitations. The Chamesian response was not simply unusual — it was unheard of. It would have been entirely appropriate for Abe to point out that he had already been approached and had made his pledge.

But Abe said not a word. He understood the enormous challenges and profound discomfort involved in fund solicitation. He saw how rabbis and educators frequently felt Lilliputian as they tried to raise support for their worthy institutions. Sparing them any sort of humiliation, from Abe's perspective, fell squarely under the rubric of *kavod haTorah* — no matter how it impacted his own wallet.

❀ THERE SHOULD BE NO GREATER SOURCE OF PLEASURE IN LIFE THAN A YOM TOV! (IF THIS IS NOT THE CASE: DO SOMETHING ABOUT IT)

Here was a man who believed in squeezing every bit of joy out of every single day. And what better opportunity could there be than *Yom Tov* — the special days appointed by the Almighty for public celebration?

Alas, however, this is a lofty theory not always supported by reality.

If there was anything Abe was, it was a realist. He saw that many kids were bored to tears (and, for that matter, so were some adults) towards the end of a week-long holiday; and he feared that if it was not enlivened, they may give in to behaviors that in no way bespoke *simchas Yom Tov.*

Once again Abe reached into his bottomless bag of tricks. He continuously concocted new ways to make the *Yomim Tovim* enjoyable, memorable and something that no one would ever want to miss. On the last day of Pesach, Abe and Deborah would host a gala barbecue in their community that was very well attended.

But that was only the tip of the (*kosher l'Pesach*) popsicle as far as *Pesachdig* entertaining. His epiphany came when he saw how hotel guests were drawn to the comforting hot drinks and the potato starch masquerading as overly-sweetened confections whenever the hotel dining room was closed. The day he realized how much people relished this (over-)indulgence, he decided to open a "Tea Room" of his own for the duration of the holiday. It was open to members of the community, to visitors — to anyone. In fact, the one year that the Chameses actually went away for Passover, he still kept his Tea Room running. He hadn't opened it for himself; it was created for others. And as people enjoyed it so much, he saw no reason to close it just because his family would be away.

The all-too-familiar phenomenon of people counting the minutes until a holiday was over simply did not exist in the Chames household. It was as true on the first day of Chanukah as it was on the last day of Pesach, and it wasn't only about gustatory pleasures. The man had an uncanny instinct for providing people with true *simchas ha'chaim,* 365 days a year — and this *totally* kicked into high gear when there was a genuine reason to celebrate. If God commanded His people to rejoice, Abe would see to it that everybody fulfilled that commandment in a BIG way.

To wit: every year the Chames' sukkah was constructed with a theme, and immense creativity was lavished upon its execution. A fabulous menu inevitably mirrored the theme, and this seasonal rite — like every Chamesian affair — garnered great anticipation and curiosity throughout the community. Naturally, like everything Abe orchestrated, it was over-the-top. And, naturally, there was a major dose of shtick.

One year the theme was "winter," which was no small challenge in sun-drenched Florida. Despite the hearty winter "comfort food" cuisine, and the various photos of Jerusalem bedecked in the white stuff, an objective outsider probably would have scored that year's theme as an "A" for concept, but a "B" for execution.

That is, until a *Shabbos*-clock activated a well-hidden SNOW MACHINE inside the sukkah. No doubt even the *ushpizin* were awestruck by the sight of snowflakes falling through the *s'chach* and drifting through the balmy Florida air. As every jaw dropped, Abe's trademark chuckle erupted into a full-bodied laugh. As always, Abe Chames thoroughly enjoyed having the last laugh. Many ran with Abe's idea of creating a sukkah theme, and nothing delighted him more. For as a result, even in the midst of hurricane season, the construction of a sukkah was never viewed as an onerous (even perhaps futile) obligation.

✿ EMBRACE ALL HUMAN BEINGS WITH RESPECT FOR THE POTENTIAL THEY POSSESS — ESPECIALLY THOSE WHO ARE YOUNG, LOST AND AT RISK — AND THEY WILL RISE TO YOUR EXPECTATIONS

The troubled teenager had lately been experiencing more than his share of confusion and angst. His parents had recently divorced, and he needed *a lot* — primarily, a father. Unable to process or articulate the pain at his core, the youth stubbornly fixated on staying in Miami and deferring (if not foregoing) his post-high-school year of learning Torah in Israel.

What was so compelling? It was the fact that the Miami Heat had just acquired his childhood sports hero: the NBA superstar, the one-and-only Shaquille O'Neal. Here was his chance to see the legendary "Shaq Attack" on his home court!

Unquestionably, the best place for this boy was away from home and learning in Israel. But if this avid sports fan spent the entire year obsessing over having missed out on Shaq heating up the *Heat*, his yeshivah experience would be wasted.

Instead of dismissing the boy's desire as juvenile and foolish, Abe instinctively knew what could be done and what a loving father would do. He made sure that every single sports magazine and newspaper clipping that featured Shaq was immediately mailed to Jerusalem via expedited service. These packages, which often also contained Miami Heat jerseys and other basketball memorabilia, turned out to be more important than anyone could have imagined. They were exactly what the boy needed in order to immerse himself successfully in his yeshivah studies, and they did wonders to raise his spirits.

Another Miami youth from a difficult family environment, Shmuel, frequently accompanied Abe to football games, where his kindly benefactor spared none of the fanfare that makes professional sports such an unforgettable experience for a wide-eyed young attendee. "We hugged when our team scored and embraced when they won, and Abe was always there for me when they lost," remembers Shmuel. "Before one game I lost my ticket in the parking lot. I thought this would be my last game with Dr. Chames... but that's because I mistakenly confused him with *other* people!

"Even when I left for yeshivah, and later college, he wanted to know when I would be coming home to join him again."

As always, Abe Chames could look into the heart of a person — especially a young person who was troubled — and see what was needed *the most.*

Said Shmuel: "Dr. Chames gave me gifts, took me places, did fun things with me, and had me over to his Shabbos table all the time, and I'll always value every opportunity I had to get close to him. But the thing that meant the most was how he greeted me. It didn't matter who was watching or where we were. *'SHMULEEE!!!'* he'd bellow out, with arms wide open, *'Gimme some LOVE!'* followed by a bear hug and some chest bumps. Nothing could have meant more to me. And just like he knew exactly how to reach *me*, he was clued in to the wavelength of many other kids..."

Young Master *Shmuleeee* was correct. Abe changed the course of young people's lives by meeting them on their own turf, showing them unconditional love, treating them as individuals and knowing exactly what they needed in order to thrive.

✿ INTEGRITY IS NOT A VIRTUE BUT RATHER A REQUIREMENT

Abe Chames had only one way of earning money: the honest way. After he passed away, letters poured in from his business associates — most of them, as it happened, non-Jews — attesting to integrity and honor that they had never witnessed in anyone else. Deborah and Abe met when they were just teenagers. She knew him like she knew her own heart. Those who saw her prostrate at the *kever* might have also heard her poignant cry: "In *Shomayim* they will have nothing to say... every single penny of yours was honest..."

Abe did not cut corners in any of his dealings. For example, Abe and Deborah disapproved of the copious amounts of alcoholic beverages that flowed all too freely at many of the *s'machos* they attended. Therefore, when they made arrangements for their son Jonathan's *aufruf,* they made it clear to the caterer that they did not want him to push the drinks. However, Abe was also cognizant that the most lucrative component of an affair was the alcohol.

Accordingly, Abe proposed that he would pay a reasonable amount per person to cover what the caterer's profit would have amounted to, had a wide variety of alcoholic beverages been made available. Over and above this, Abe stipulated that he would pay for every bottle of wine that was uncorked at the bar, regardless of whether or not it was finished. This way the caterer would have no financial incentive to promote the consumption of alcohol.

After Deborah had settled all of the expenses, Abe asked whether the caterer had charged for the bottles. Deborah said he had not, and Abe sent her back to pay for what had been agreed upon. She was a bit puzzled by his insistence on this count, for she didn't grasp why it was necessary to pay for the bottles in addition to the price per head for something that they neither wanted nor consumed. But Abe reverted to his *"nuthin' doin'"* stance. "I don't want the caterer to short-change himself," he said emphatically, "and there is absolutely no reason that our particular desires should impinge upon his *parnassah*. Further," he told her, "I gave my word." And although it was clear that the caterer had forgotten, Abe had not.

The caterer gawked at Deborah in disbelief. "Never," the man said all incredulity, "has someone ever come back after a bill has been settled to pay extra! How much more so to insist on paying for what I never insisted upon nor requested."

The aphorism "you can't take it with you," was one that Abe lived by; nothing made him happier than to give. And yet he left this world with steamer trunks laden with priceless *mitzvos* and countless *chassadim*.

❀ IF YOU RADIATE HAPPINESS AND OPTIMISM, YOUR COMPANY WILL BE A PLEASURE — AND YOUR POSITIVE ENERGY WILL BE CONTAGIOUS

Let's be frank: the very word "carpool" reeks of tedium for both the adult driver and the child passengers. But *not* carpooling Abe-Chames-style. Regularly, this busiest of men would help out families in the neighborhood by doing some of their driving. Dreary trips home after long, tiring school days turned into rollicking adventures when Dr. Chames was in the driver's seat. Lively Jewish music blasting from the cd player (this was not your father's bad-news news radio), mandated stops at the 7-11 or the donut shop (this was not your mother's lengthy list of dreary errands), liberty to chow down on the after-school treat of your choice (forget the no-snack rule), free rein — within the parameters of safety, of course — to act a little nutty and a lot noisy (forget the *'zei shtill!'* rule).

Maybe the kids all loved him because they instinctively sensed that Abe — who had *sifre kodesh* lovingly wedged between Mickey Mouse bookends on his library shelf — was, at heart, a big, overgrown kid himself, profoundly in touch with the most precious (even holy) parts of being a child which most adults, sadly, leave behind: utter spontaneity, guileless enthusiasm, infectious joy, affection for others that is unhampered by egotism and unsullied by "agendas"; the pleasure of a good joke and the unselfconscious ability to be silly, especially if it can bring a smile to the lips of one who really needs a smile.

Abe was the only parent in America, perhaps the world, that youngsters liked as much as their peers. Kids would come over to play with the boys, but equally enjoyed hanging out with Dr. Chames. And this refers to children of all ages and stripes.

Here are the fond recollections of one of them. Today, she is almost a grown-up; but when she first climbed anxiously into Dr. Chames' minivan, she was a shy third-grader, new to the neighborhood:

"We piled into the car and the seemingly too-happy-for-his-own-good driver headed in the direction of home. Each kid in the carpool seemed to have a joke with Dr. Chames or, as they called him, 'Abe.'

"I remember being shocked that children were allowed to call this doctor by his first name, but I soon realized why: everyone in the car giggled when he said anything. We soon pulled up to a red light on the corner of 10th Avenue. Abe saw that the public high school was also letting out. He turned his head around, gave a big smile to all of us and said "1... 2... 3... GO!" Suddenly the car began to rock. All of the kids bounced up and down as Abe jumped up and down in his seat. I looked out the window and saw about 50 pairs of eyes staring at the car, which looked like a ship in rocky waters. The car swayed from right to left over and over again, like the gyration in a washing machine agitator. I tried to duck so nobody outside would see me, but the kids in the car were *laughing so hard I thought their jaws would get locked!*

"*Before I knew it, I began to laugh too, but it was a different type of laughter. It was a nervous laugh, a laugh out of shock. I was nervous that this crazy man named Abe wouldn't get me home safely. The laugh began to switch when I observed how an adult had such an amazing way of making kids happy. And then my laughter became thoroughly genuine when I realized that I had just made a new friend named Abe.*

"*And as quickly as it started, it ended. The light turned green, and we drove home with smiles frozen on our faces.*

"*Abe not only got me home safely, but he also left me with a memory that will never leave me. A memory of the first time I didn't care what anyone outside the car thought. A memory of the first time I felt like part of the community, because we all had a special bond — a friendship with Abe. A memory of the first time I met this special man who lived to make other people happy, and who did an exceedingly good job.*"

Abe's *shtick* was not only limited to the kids. There is surely no one else who sent birthday cards to *rebbeim* in the yeshivah; and positively *no one* who ever dreamed of "showin' some love" by sending them... Valentine's Day (!) cards. No one could help bursting into laughter when the perpetrator of the joke was their good (and good-hearted) friend Abe.

Abe's daughter Melissa recalls coming upon him holding court in a vestibule at a wedding, surrounded by a gaggle of giggling *rebbetzins*. He was regaling them with his over-the-top jokes and clearly not a one could maintain her composure. "Uh, what's going on?" asked Melissa as she beheld this somewhat unusual scene.

Abe waved her off with assurance. "It's under control," he declared, and the gales of laughter erupted anew.

At *s'machos* the *rebbeim* would insist on being seated with him — not because he was a big philanthropist, but because they deeply enjoyed being with him and cherished his company. At one such gathering, one of them was heard to say: "Put the *Rosh*

Yeshivah next to Abe — let him have a good time for once!"

The fact is, everyone liked to be in Abe's company. Who wouldn't want to be around someone who was always happy and unconditionally loving? Even his correspondence bespoke unabashed good cheer and affection. "Love and kisses," he would sign his letters and e-mails, even to new acquaintances, often adding "xoxo" as youngsters more commonly do.

✿ HUMOR IS A BLESSING, BUT NEVER AT ANY-ONE'S EXPENSE; AND WHEN YOU GIVE, GIVE WITH A SMILE

Abe was a remarkably intelligent and astute man, but he never made anyone feel foolish or ignorant — even with all of his trademark joking and teasing. No one ever misunderstood his ribbing as anything other than a confirmation of his genuine affection.

One had to get up very early to dupe Dr. Chames — but invariably, it was never early enough. I myself once tried to put one over on the master, and was actually acquiring a heady feeling of victory — but alas, it was premature. We were dining in a Manhattan restaurant and I (thought I had) succeeded in surreptitiously informing the waiter — in hushed tones and out of everyone's sight — that the meal was on me. Knowing who I was up against, I even made the waiter give me his solemn word that he would give *me* the check, and we shook on it.

But at the end of our most enjoyable evening, the same waiter blithely placed a receipt in front of Abe; the bill had already been run through on his credit card. I was one-upped! I glowered at the waiter and was prepared to register my protest, when the look he gave me stopped me in my tracks. It was this matter-of-fact, *"you-stupid-or-something??"* look, and it pretty much summed up the reality. How did I have the temerity to think that Abe Chames and I were in the same league? All right, maybe there was a crisp Ulysses S. Grant tucked neatly inside the waiter's back pocket; but in any case, I learned my lesson: don't mess with Big Abe.

Rabbi Zev Leff said at the funeral that the Almighty wanted Abe's beautiful smile to be with Him in Heaven. As painful as it is to be without Abe, who died suddenly on the ninth of Kislev, 2008, at the age of 54, there is a modicum of comfort knowing that he will undoubtedly still be working on behalf of his People. He never shied away from a challenge in this world and there is no reason to suspect that he will do so in the next. No one who knew Abe has any problem picturing him going before the Heavenly Assembly and vehemently arguing: *"Nuthin' doin'!"*

Because of his single-minded pursuit of *chessed* he was enabled to accomplish in a relatively brief time on earth, what a cadre of individuals could not possibly dream of achieving even in the fullness of years. Abe's sudden and untimely death, it must be said, should serve as a clarion call to each and every one of us, not to tarry in establishing our own legacy of good deeds. Delay and procrastination were completely unknown to this man, who consistently gave of himself today, as if there were no tomorrow...

⚘ LAST, BUT NEVER, EVER LEAST: WHILE SPREADING SUNSHINE AND *MITZVOS*, START IN YOUR OWN BACKYARD

Even with the round-the-clock demands of his profession and his community work, Abe Chames enjoyed the greatest blessing of all: a family life that was abundant with the type of unadulterated joy he spread — thanks to his devoted wife, Deborah, who was his partner in everything that he did. She continues his legacy, but not singlehandedly. The Chames children, Melissa, Jonathan and Jacob, along with their spouses, are imbued with the warm and loving spirits of both their parents.

Abe was a doting and mirthful father, but this did not mean he took the role of parent lightly. He loved his children too much for that.

To do for others was his creed. Since his passing, the question is repeated on so many lips: "What would Abe do?" Here, then, you now have an Operator's Manual for "The World According to Abe". And as the great Talmudic sage Hillel proclaimed (Shabbos 31), *"Zil u'gmar* — Go out and learn it."

Imagine, just imagine, if we all lived in "The World According to Abe." A world in which all physical ailments and pain are attended to swiftly and expertly, stripping no one of dignity. A world in which the spirit, *the pintele Yid* in each Jew, no matter how hard to reach, is nurtured with endless tenderness and compassion. A world governed by his mantra, "treat others, as you wish to be treated." A world of magical snow-showers inside sukkahs, fairly recompensed *melamdim* at gorgeous, ornate tables where they teach eager yeshiva *bochrim,* and "no Jewish child left behind" when the destination is Disney World. A world where every mitzvah is done beautifully to the hilt, where *tzedakah* is quiet and matter-of-fact, and where laughter shines steadfastly even through tears. Where every letter ends with "Love and Kisses," and every road leads to a house with an open door, where the Tea Room is open 24/7 and good people gather to praise *Hashem*'s name.

This is the house that Abraham Chames built; and as God promised *Avraham Avinu*, the patriarch Abraham:

"I shall make thy name great."

Glossary

Glossary

The following glossary provides a partial explanation of some of the foreign words and phrases used in this book. The spelling, tense, and explanations reflect the way the specific word is used in *TOO BEAUTIFUL*. Often, there are alternate spellings and meanings for the words. Foreign words and phrases which are immediately followed by a translation in the text are not included in this section.

A"H (ALE'HA HASHALOM): may she rest in peace.

AFILU B'CHADREI CHADORIM: even in private.

ALIYAH: lit. ascent; immigration to ERETZ YIS-RAEL.

ALIYAH LA'REGEL: classically the pilgrimage to Jerusalem in honor of the holidays (Pesach, Shavuos, Sukkos).

ARON(OT) KODESH: lit. holy ark; ark containing the Torah scrolls.

AUFRUF: a celebration traditionally held for a groom on the SHABBOS preceding his wedding.

AVEL (AVEILIM): mourner(s).

AVOS U'VANIM: father-son learning program.

AVRAHAM AVINU: our forefather, Abraham.

AVREICH: young married yeshivah student.

AZKARA: memorial.

B'SHA'A TOVA UMUTZLACHAS: lit. in a good and successful hour; expresses hope that the time of a particular event will be propitious.

BAAL HABAYIS: layperson.

BAAL HASIMCHA: one who hosts a celebration.

BAAL TOKEI'AH: one who blows the shofar.

BACHUR(IM): unmarried yeshivah student(s).

BADAT"Z: the Jerusalem Rabbinical court.

BAYIS NE'EMAN B'YISRAEL: blessing customarily given to newlywed couple.

BEIN ADAM L'CHAVEIRO: between man and his fellow.

BEIN ADAM L'MAKOM: between man and God.

BEIS AVEL: house of mourning.

BEIS MEDRASH: house of Torah study.

BEN TORAH: lit. son of Torah; person imbued with Torah values and committed to its study.

BIRKAS HACHAMA: blessing upon the sun, recited once every 28 years.

BRACHA: blessing.

BRACHA L'VATALAH: gratuitous, hence insulting blessing.

BRIS MILAH: the Jewish rite of circumcision.

CHANUKAH GELT: money distributed to children on Chanukah.

CHAS V'CHALILAH: God forbid.

CHAVRUSA: Torah study partner.

CHESSED (CHASSADIM): loving-kindness(es).

CHAZZAN: cantor; the leader of public worship.

DAYAN: a rabbinical judge.

EIDEM: (Y.) son in law.

EIRUV: a wire suspended around an area to permit carrying within that area on Shabbos.

ELUL: the last Hebrew month, corresponding to August/September.

ERETZ YISRAEL: the Land of Israel.

EREV: eve.

GABBAI (GABBA'IM): functionary of the synagogue.

GABBAI TZEDAKAH: one in charge of charity funds.

GADOL: lit. great one; refers to a giant in Torah scholarship.

GADOL HADOR: greatest Torah scholar of the generation.

GAON(IM): lit. brilliant one; honorific for a distinguished sage.

GARTEL: (Y.) belt worn by some men during prayer.

GLATT: (Y.) strictly kosher.

GVIR: man of substantial means.

HAKAFOS: circuits.

HALACHA (HALACHOS): Jewish law(s).

HASHAVAS AVEIDAH: returning a lost object.

HASHEM: God.

HETTER: halachic dispensation.

HATZOLAH: work involving saving lives.

IM YIRTZEH HASHEM: please God.

ISRU CHAG: the day following a holiday.

IVRIT: Hebrew.

IYAR: the Hebrew month corresponding to April/May.

K'DARKO: in his usual manner.

K'SHMAH KEIN HEE: her name depicts what she is.

KALLAH: bride.

KALLAH IZ ZU SHEIN: (Y.) The bride is too beautiful!

KASHER: to make kosher.

KASHRUS: conforming to Jewish dietary regulations

KAVOD HATORAH: lit. "the Torah's honor," the respect given to the Torah.

KEDUSHAH: holiness.

KEHILLA: congregation.

KEVER: grave.

KIDDUSH: blessing sanctifying the Sabbath, usually recited over a cup of wine.

KIPPAH (KIPPOS): skullcap(s).

KIRUV RECHOKIM: drawing non-observant Jews closer to Torah observance.

KLALL: community.

KLALL YISRAEL: community of Israel; all of Jewry.

KOLLEL: post-graduate yeshivah in which the student body is usually comprised of young married men who receive stipends.

KOVEAH ITTIM: set aside time (for Torah study).

KRIAS HATORAH: Torah reading.

KVATTER: one honored with escorting the baby during the BRIS MILAH ceremony.

MAARIV: the evening prayer service.

MAGGID: itinerant storyteller who speaks publicly to inspire and rebuke.

MAKOM SHENAHAGU: the customs and laws of one's current locale must be adopted.

MANHIG: a leader.

MASMID: diligent student.

MEHUDAR: especially beautiful.

MELACHAH: lit. work; the thirty-nine types of work forbidden on the Sabbath.

MELAMED (MELAMDIM): teacher(s).

MENACHEM AVEL: a condolence call to comfort the bereaved.

MESHULACH (MESHULACHIM): lit. agent(s); fundraiser(s).

MIKVA(MIKVAOS): a ritual bath used for the purpose of ritual purification.

MINCHAH: the afternoon prayer service.

MITZVOS: commandments.

MOHEL(IM): one who performs the religious ceremony of circumcision.

MOTZA'EI SHABBOS: Saturday night.

MOTZA'EI SHAVUOS: the night following the holiday of Shavuos.

MUSSAR: (the study of) ethics

❦

NEBBACH: (Y.) unfortunately.

NETILAS YADAYIM: ritual washing of hands.

NU: (Y.) Well?

❦

OILEM: lit. world; colloq. group of similar persuasion.

OLEH REGEL: one who performs the pilgrimage of ALIYAH LA'REGEL.

❦

PARNASSAH: livelihood.

PAYOS: sidelocks; long, usually curly sidelocks worn by Chassidim.

PESACH: Passover.

PESACHDIG: (Y.) kosher for Pesach.

PIKUACH NEFESH: saving a life.

PINTELE YID: (Y.) the spark of Jewish identity.

POSEIK: one who renders halachic decisions.

PSAK: halachic decision.

❦

RAMBAM: Maimonides.

RASHI: leading commentator on the Bible and Talmud.

RAV: rabbi.

REB: (Y.) respectful form of address.

REBBE(IM): (Y.) rabbi(s); Torah teacher(s); Chassidic leader(s).

REBBETZIN: (Y.) rabbi's wife.

ROSH YESHIVAH: the dean of a yeshivah.

S'CHACH: the roof of a Sukkah, generally made from branches or bamboo.

SANDAK: individual who holds the baby during the circumcision.

SEFER (SEFARIM): book(s); sacred book(s).

SEFER (SIFREI) TORAH: Torah scroll(s).

SEMICHAH: rabbinical ordination.

SEUDAH (SEUDOS): festive meal(s).

SEUDAS MITZVAH: festive meal held after a mitzvah ceremony.

SHABBATON: a gathering or convocation centered around SHABBOS.

SHABBOS(OS): the Sabbath(s).

SHACHARIS: morning prayer service.

SHAILA (SHAILOS): (Y.) halachic question(s).

SHAITEL MACHER: (Y.) wig stylist.

SHALIACH MITZVAH: an emissary for a mitzvah.

SHALOM BAYIS: marital harmony.

SHOMAYIM: Heaven.

SHEHAKOL: blessing recited before eating certain types of food.

SHEMA: prayer proclaiming God's oneness.

SHEVA BRACHOS: the seven benedictions recited at a wedding; one of the festive meals held in honor of the bride and groom during the week following the wedding, at which these blessings are recited.

SHEVAT: the Hebrew month corresponding to January/February.

SHIDDUCH(IM): (marital) match(es).

SHIR HAMAALOS: a Psalm sung before Grace After Meals.

SHIUR: Torah lecture.

SHIVA: lit. seven; the seven-day mourning period following the death of an immediate relative.

SHLEMAZEL: (Y.) one who has bad luck.

SHLEMIEL: (Y.) colloq. the cause of misfortune.

SHMUZ(EN): ethical discourse(s).

SHOCHET: ritual slaughterer.

SHTIEBEL (SHTIEBLACH): (Y.) small, informal, intimate room(s) for prayer or study.

SHTICKEL: (Y) a little.

SHTREIMEL: (Y.) decorative fur or fur-trimmed hat worn by male Chassidim on Sabbath and festivals.

SHUL: (Y.) synagogue.

SHULCHAN: table.

SIFREI KODESH: sacred books.

SIMCHA (S'MACHOS): lit. joy; celebration.

SIMCHAS HA'CHAIM: *joie-de-vivre.*

SIMCHAS TORAH: the holiday of rejoicing over the Torah.

SUKKAH: temporary dwelling which is a central requirement of the Sukkos holiday.

TALLIS (TALLEISIM): four-cornered prayer shawl with fringes at each corner, worn by men during morning prayers.

TALMID CHACHAM: scholar, learned man.

TEFILLAH: prayer

TEFILLIN: black leather boxes containing verses from the Bible, bound to a man's arm and the front of his head during morning prayers.

TEHILLIM: Psalms.

TESHUVAH(OS): halachic responsum (responsa).

TICHEL: (Y.) headscarf.

TOSAFOS: medieval annotations and commentaries on the Talmud.

TZADDEKES: righteous woman.

TZEDAKA: charity.

USHPIZIN: spiritual guests that are summoned to the SUKKAH.

VUSS KEN ICH MACHEN: (Y.) What can I do?

YAD: silver ornament used to point to the text of the Torah scroll during public readings.

YAHRZEIT: (Y.) anniversary of a death.

YESHIVAH BACHUR: unmarried yeshivah student.

YIDDISHE NESHAMOS: (Y.) Jewish souls.

YIRAS SHOMAYIM: fear of Heaven.

YOM(IM) TOV(IM): holiday(s).

YOM TOV SHEINI: the second day of a holiday observed only by those outside of ERETZ YISRAEL.

YOMIM NORAIM: the High Holy days.

YOTZEI: fulfilled my obligation

ZECHUS: merit.

ZEI SHTILL: (Y.) be quiet.

Z"L (ZICHRONAM LIVRACHA): of blessed memory.

ZT"L (ZECHER TZADDIK LIVRACHA): may the memory of a righteous one be a blessing.

Inspiring, superbly written contemporary literature for every Jewish family
by the award-winning author, lecturer and educator

HANOCH TELLER

SHORT STORIES

ONCE UPON A SOUL
Twenty-five powerful true stories which fascinate, inspire, and enrich the soul. 221 pp.

SOUL SURVIVORS
In these true stories, the mighty hand of the Almighty reaches out to His faithful wherever they may be. 286 pp.

"SOULED!"
Book I – Adult tales of altruism, salvation, and serendipity. Book II – Legend and lore for children. 384 pp.

PICHIFKES
STORIES HEARD ON THE ROAD AND BY THE WAY
This great anthology is liberally seasoned with precious, insightful lessons in life. 245 pp.

HEY, TAXI!
Heart-warming "soul stories" heard in taxies or told by cabbies all over the world. 384 pp.

COURTROOMS OF THE MIND
Twenty true-to-life cases where the only defense witnesses are the heart and soul. 288 pp.

ABOVE THE BOTTOM LINE
Stories of integrity that portray God's aversion to deception, and teach us to rise above expediency. 413 pp.

GIVE PEACE A STANCE
Stories which promote peaceful relationships and means of avoiding strife. Plus an exposé on a well-known cult. 344 pp.

IT'S A SMALL WORD AFTER ALL
Stories that highlight the amazing impact of a kind gesture or a thoughtful remark on human lives and events. 444 pp.

IN AN UNRELATED STORY
A compelling collection of news-worthy tales that teach and touch. 318 pp.

Edifying BIOGRAPHIES, thought-provoking ESSAYS and entertaining STORIES FOR YOUTH – quoted by religious leaders and laymen, politicians and the man on the street. For a truly unique reading experience there's nothing like a book by

HANOCH TELLER

BIOGRAPHIES

SUNSET. Instructive and dramatic episodes in the lives of ten contemporary Torah luminaries. Revised and enlarged edition. 288 pp.

THE BOSTONER. Stories and recollection from the colorful court of the Bostoner Rebbe, Rabbi Levi I. Horowitz, whose philanthropic and outreach endeavors have earned international acclaim. 209 pp.

BRIDGES OF STEEL, LADDERS OF GOLD. The rags-to-riches story of philanthropist Joseph Tanenbaum, who endowed over 1,000 Jewish educational institutions.

A MATTER OF PRINCIPAL. The fascinating biography of the renowned educator, Rabbi Binyamin Steinberg, *z"l*, principal of Bais Yaakov of Baltimore and champion of women's education in the U.S. 296 pp.

AND FROM JERUSALEM, HIS WORD. An inspiring tribute to the beloved gadol ha-dor, Rabbi Shlomo Zalman Auerbach *zt"l*, whose vast scope and legacy of Torah knowledge, humility and love of chesed affected Jews the world over. 399. pp.

PARSHAS HASHAVUA

A MIDRASH AND A MAASEH. An anthology of insights and commentatries on the weekly Torah reading, including hundreds of old favorites and new stories. 2 volumes, slip-cased, 1,006 pp.

YOUNG READERS

THE BEST OF STORYLINES. Over two dozen inspiring stories that convey Jewish values and Torah concepts. 224 pp.

WELCOME TO THE REAL WORLD. The story of a young girl's rite of passage as she faces the first real challenges of her life.

Comprehending the Incomprehensible

This series is a riveting and enlightening history of the Holocaust by one of Yad Vashem's most celebrated docents. For over two decades Hanoch Teller has been guiding youth and adults through the darkest period in history making his tour of Yad Vashem an unforgettable life milestone.

This eleven-part lecture series leads the listener through the halls of Yad Vashem into the bowels of the Holocaust; from seething Germany in the thirties to apathetic America in the forties; from the murder apparatus in Poland to the rescue efforts in Switzerland. For one who wishes to learn and understand what really occurred there is nothing as compelling, lucid, concise and insightful.

Each of the lectures has been recorded in a studio at the highest-fidelity. Thirteen hours of captivating listening encompasses the historical events and personal accounts of survivors before and during the war years, providing an in-depth analysis of the political, social, religious and moral issues affecting perpetrators and victims, collaborators and resisters, apologists and rescue workers.

The Sound of Soul

The Sound of Soul Volumes I & II provide over two hours of listening enjoyment for the entire family. The most heart-warming, enlightening, hilarious and poignant of Teller's tales have been transformed into an audio classic, fully dramatized, with musical accompaniment and vivid sound effects. Joy and drama, laughter and pathos combine to convey the timeless precepts of Judaism to young and old alike.

Available through
www.hanochteller.com

Do You Believe in
MIRACLES?

When events occur that defy all laws of nature and reason, you know you are witnessing a miracle. In this widely-acclaimed, award-winning, *New York Times* **Critic's Choice** 65-minute docu-drama, Hanoch Teller presents incredible-but-true miraculous events in the lives of ordinary people – powerful evidence of the Almighty's constant involvement in mankind's existence. These heart-warming episodes, re-enacted by top performers, fully orchestrated by leading musicians and enhanced by state-of-the-art graphics and effects, are a celebration of Divine Providence and Jewish pride. Acclaimed by educators as the most important and vital Jewish teaching tool of this decade, and a *kiruv* vehicle second to none - "Miracles" is a masterpiece of inspiration that viewers of all ages will cherish for a lifetime and families will want to see again and again.

You'll laugh - you'll cry - you'll stand up and cheer - and most of all... you'll BELIEVE!

The Righteous Live On

The Righteous Live On series explores the life and the times, the challenges and the achievements of many of our great luminaries, who made such a powerful impact upon the generation, that their stories are fundamental knowledge for the Torah-conscientious Jew.

With a wealth of erudition, history, humor and pathos, Rabbi Hanoch Teller tells these critical tales as no one else can. These lectures are required listening for adults and youth, from the staunchly observant to those with nominal knowledge and religious commitment.

Available through
www.hanochteller.com

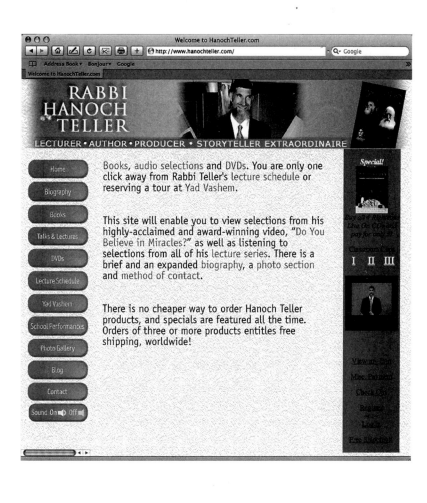